22 (copenhagen)
70-74 (opera occasions)

SPEAK
AS A
LEADER

ALSO BY HERMAN CAIN

Leadership Is Common Sense

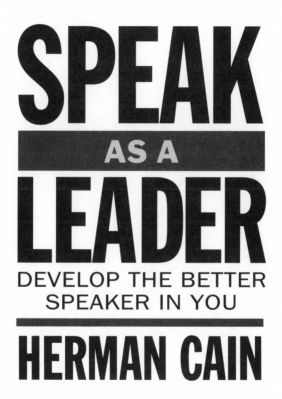

SPEAK
AS A
LEADER

DEVELOP THE BETTER
SPEAKER IN YOU

HERMAN CAIN

LEBHAR-FRIEDMAN BOOKS

New York • Chicago • Los Angeles • London • Paris • Tokyo

Lebhar-Friedman Books
425 Park Avenue
New York, NY 10022

Published by Lebhar-Friedman Books
Lebhar-Friedman Books is a company of Lebhar-Friedman, Inc.

Printed in the United States of America

Library of Congress Cataloging-in-Publication Data

Cain, Herman.
    Speak as a leader / Herman Cain.
        p.   cm.
    Includes bibliographical references and index.
    ISBN 0-86730-782-X
    1. Public speaking.   2. Leadership.   I. Title.
PN4121.C224   1999   99-30476
808.5'1—dc21   CIP

Text design by Tina Thompson

Volume Discounts

This book makes a great gift and incentive. Call
(212) 756-5240 for information on volume discounts.

To my parents,
Luther and Lenora Cain,
for insisting that I go to church as a child

CONTENTS

ACKNOWLEDGMENTS

To Gloria Cain, my wife, for allowing my creative writing time to intrude on "her time";

Kathleen Sullivan, for encouraging me to do this project by constantly reminding me that a real author has more than just one book;

Sibby Wolfson for typing my endless drafts and changes and for giving me her suggestions whether I wanted them or not;

Melissa Rosati, for helping me to make this a great book;

Geoff Golson, my publisher at Lebhar-Friedman Books, for his encouragement and for his supportive staff;

And all the audiences who helped me to develop the *better speaker in me.*

My sincere *thanks* to all of you.

FOREWORD
by Dr. Robert H. Schuller

Herman Cain is a dreamer.

Early in life, by his father's example, Herman learned that dreams empower one with self-motivation to take on personal and professional challenges. Luther Cain, Jr., worked three jobs to provide for his family. The first job paid the rent. The second job put food on the table, and the money from the third job was dedicated to the purchase of a family home. It was a small brick house with indoor plumbing, and it was Luther Cain's greatest dream.

Herman's dreams—to take care of his family, to build great companies and organizations, and to serve others in pursuit of their dreams—continue to motivate him. "Success is a journey and not a destination" is one of his most deeply held beliefs. In *Speak as a Leader: Develop the Better Speaker in You,* Herman illustrates that we all have the potential to dream and to become more effective as leaders and communicators in our society.

Herman understands that leadership is hard work and that it is based on inspiring people to perform to the best of their ability. People do not want to be told what to do. They want to be led by leaders who are sincere and credible in their personal and professional lives. As one of my guests on the *Hour of Power,* Herman shared with millions of people the story of Godfather's Pizza and its goal to have employees who are in their souls and hearts "exceptionally wonderful." This trait is found in the highest quality ingredients that make an excellent product. More important, the customer—who is the lifeblood of the business—recognizes this trait.

Speak as a Leader is a book of practical techniques to help you become a better communicator. Some of the examples will make you laugh. Some of them will touch you deeply. Within the pages of this book, Herman challenges you with the questions for reflection. Be ready to make the time to practice his suggestions and to become your own toughest critic. When I read his words, I hear his glorious baritone voice, and you will too.

I supported Herman Cain's nomination for membership in the Horatio Alger Association, where he was elected and installed in 1996. He earned this award, and I am proud of him! And he is the only CEO I know who is a gospel music performer and recording artist. Wow!

Dear reader, turn the pages and become acquainted with one of America's power thinkers, who has an inspiring, positive, fantastic message for everyone who wants to communicate effectively in any private or public speaking situation.

PREFACE

This book is a keynote speech about public speaking. Listen closely as you read and you will discover the relationship between your leadership skills and your public speaking ability. Visualize yourself in the situation described and practice the techniques herein and you will release the better speaker in you.

First Things First

Leaders make things happen by *removing* barriers to self-motivation, *obtaining* results for the right problems, and *inspiring* people to exceed their expectations. These are the *three critical things* that a leader *must* do. Noted author Joel Barker defines a leader as someone who takes people to where they would not go by themselves. Similarly, speakers cause people to *think* where they would not think by themselves by using the power of the spoken word. A poor speaker never gains the audience's attention, and consequently, the goal of the speech is never achieved. When a great speaker is before an audience, the speech makes a *connection* with the audience and the words inspire the listeners to change or crystallize their thinking in unlimited ways.

The power of the spoken word has been challenged throughout history but never subjugated. When properly conceived, organized, researched, written, and delivered, the spoken word penetrates the mind and the heart, which inspires people to change their behavior, their attitude, and sometimes their lives. For example, I do not recall anyplace in the New Testament where Jesus Christ was singing or dancing in an attempt to convince people to change their behavior. Can you? No. He *spoke* and his words changed the world. None of us possesses the rhetorical power of Jesus, but all of us can harness the strength of the spoken word.

Leaders use the power of the spoken word to inspire people beyond their expectations. First, you must learn to visualize and to think of yourself as a leader before you will be able to "speak as a leader" effectively. Throughout the course of our hectic lives, each one of us becomes a leader in one way or another. When a speaker has the podium, microphone, or attention of the audience, he or she is the leader at that moment. This book, this keynote, if you will, is designed to inspire you to develop your leadership skills and to learn how to create a meaningful message in the minds and hearts of your audience.

This book is not based on theory, it is based on practice, practice, and more practice, even though it intersects with theory quite well. Just as a doctor practices medicine and a lawyer practices law, I have practiced speaking and have evolved as a speaker ever since I gave my first speech at age ten at a church program. In fact, I still remember that first speech. The audience found it entertaining, and I was exhilarated from the audience's reaction and vigorous applause. From that day on, the members of the church who heard me were convinced I was going to be a preacher or president of the United States. At fifty-three years of age, it's not too late for either one.

As I discuss in Chapter One, *I believe that great leaders are born and good leaders are made.* Leaders lead with logically reasoned decisions derived from information, research, and knowledge. But things do not happen until the leader *speaks* to set direction, initiate action, or stimulate activity.

What better example of a born great leader than one of the most admired and respected presidents in our history, Abraham Lincoln. Lincoln is the most studied president in American history, but I have yet to read a book or article that suggests Lincoln took a leadership seminar. And even more amazing, as Donald T. Phillips noted in his *Lincoln on Leadership,* "Lincoln was viewed by his own advisors as nothing more than a gawky, second-rate country lawyer with no leadership experience." Maybe someone forgot to tell Lincoln that he was not supposed to succeed at reuniting the United States of America, and that he was not supposed to sign the Emancipation Proclamation. Great leaders instinctively possess and demonstrate the "three plus three" leadership principles described throughout this book, whereas good leaders have to work at them.

"Three plus three" refers to the *three critical qualities*—the D, E, and F factors—a leader must possess and the *three critical things*—ROI—a leader must do. A leader must have the ability to recognize that people must motivate themselves (D factor), the ability to take risks and make the tough decisions (E factor), and the ability to block out the unnecessary and concentrate on the necessary (F factor). I call these the D, E, and F factors (Drucker, entrepreneurial, and focus). The three critical things a leader must do (ROI) are *remove* barriers to motivation, *obtain* the right results by working on the right problems, and *inspire* the passion within people to perform better than expected.

As I explain in Chapter Two, learning to give an effective speech is much like learning how to swim. Namely, most of us would drown if we jumped into deep water before we learned the fundamentals of swimming. And, as in swimming, not all of us could win an Olympic gold medal no matter how long we practice, but we *can* learn how to keep from "drowning" in front of an audience.

Speaking is analogous to leading in several ways. First, you must remove the barriers to communicating your message to the audience. Second, you must obtain the desired result by delivering your message with impact and the passion of your conviction. Third, the impact of your message must inspire the listeners to change, accelerate, or eliminate some previously intended actions, attitudes, or behaviors.

Great speakers are born and good speakers are made. It just takes preparation and practice. Most of us can be good speakers, and good speakers can also achieve great things. Consider for a moment the following examples.

Abraham Lincoln was a great leader and a great speaker who was known for his thought-provoking logic and his ability to captivate an audience. He did not have radio, television, or the Internet to help inspire his audiences. His ideas, ideals, and deeds were perpetuated through his unique ability to not only write effectively but also to motivate people by the way in which he spoke to them. Similar to Lincoln, and another personal favorite of mine, is Barbara Jordan, former congresswoman from Texas. She was born a great speaker and leader. Her articulate and captivating command of the English language to express positions and conclusions of logic is unsurpassed in the modern age.

Unlike Lincoln or Jordan, Mohandas Gandhi was a great leader who was not known as a particularly great speaker. If Richard Attenborough's movie approximated what he was really like, he was able to inspire people more with his principles and unwavering beliefs than with a powerful delivery. But again, it was the way he put the words together that motivated his followers to change their lives. Because we live in the Internet age, you can see and judge Gandhi for yourself. The reference for Gandhi's radio address is included in the Internet Resource Guide in Appendix E.

At this point, I would like you to consider why it is no accident that many well-known speakers are ministers. It is because they have more opportunity to practice the art of speaking than the rest of us. As I explain in Chapters Three and Four, the more you practice, the better you will be able to speak as a confident leader. For example, Dr. Martin Luther King, Jr., was a great leader and a great speaker. He sharpened his speaking skills as a Baptist preacher before he became the civil rights leader of the century. Reverend Jesse Jackson is a great orator capable of bringing attention to an issue and igniting an audience's passion. His poetic speaking style is what motivates his audiences to listen to his message. Also, Dr. Robert Schuller is a great leader and a great speaker. He built a world ministry from a drive-in theater and inspires millions of people every week in a succinct and powerful way. He has always been one of my leadership and speaking heroes from the very first time I heard him speak.

If you use this book as a tool to sharpen your leadership and speaking abilities, you will notice a difference in audience response and in your self-confidence. Use the Development Guide, Evaluation Form, Quick Tips, and Bibliographical References to help you polish your speaking abilities. A good speech, with proper preparation using these simple techniques, will keep you from drowning in front of an audience. For example, the Quick Tips section is a handy reference guide for preparing speeches for different occasions. The Development Guide provides preparation checklists to help you prepare your speech. The Evaluation Form helps you evaluate other speeches you hear. If you really want to improve at speaking, you can, and you can work at it even while you are listening to someone else.

Good leaders who become better speakers achieve better results because of the power of the spoken word. Not everyone can achieve greatness in speaking, but everyone can become a good speaker. We can all speak as a leader.

Prepare to meet the *better speaker in you.*

SPEAK
AS A
LEADER

CHAPTER 1

Think Before You Speak

"What we have to learn to do, we learn by doing."
—ARISTOTLE (384–322 BC)

I BELIEVE THAT GREAT LEADERS
are born and good leaders are made. But I also believe that this is only
the beginning of the meaning of leadership. Throughout world history, great leaders, from Joan of Arc to Dr. Martin Luther King, Jr.,
knew instinctively how to inspire people using the power and beauty
of the spoken word. Great leaders possess critical characteristics common to all of us, and they demonstrate these qualities consistently in
their lives. They become great speakers to us when we connect with
something they say that causes us to think and believe beyond our
status quo and current expectations. Great speakers open our eyes to
possibilities that will transform our dreams into the brilliance of reality. During these shared moments with the audience, a great speaker
becomes a great leader; and a good speech that is delivered with the
passion of one's conviction becomes a great speech and a memorable
event in our lives.

THINK AS A LEADER

There is no magic formula for leadership in the 1,400 leadership books available on the market or the 3.5 million leadership references posted on the Internet. We live in a competitive, high-tech society where too many people no longer trust their natural talents and instincts. They search continuously for the right answer because they think the "right" answer must come from somewhere or someone else. I believe that we all possess qualities that those books and references may help us develop, but the difference between a great leader and a good leader is one of natural talent and desire.

From my experiences as a business leader and keynote speaker, I have learned that *leadership is common sense.* Leadership qualities exist in all of us within our hearts and minds, but those critical qualities of leadership must be cultivated. I call these qualities the *D, E,* and *F factors.* When you self-reflect and understand these factors, you will be better able to isolate your own leadership experiences and then use these experiences to speak as a leader when communicating your messages to your audience. You do not have to be a great leader to deliver a great speech, but it helps to think as a leader.

The Drucker Factor

In the field of management, no author is more prolific than Peter Drucker. While he has written hundreds of articles and numerous books, I cannot say that I have read them all or followed all his accomplishments closely. At the beginning of my career, I did have the good fortune, however, to participate in one of his leadership seminars. Like the other young managers in the room, I wanted to climb the corporate ladder and become an executive. This was my dream as well as my family's dream for me. About halfway through the seminar, Mr. Drucker said, *"You cannot motivate people. People must motivate them-*

selves." This statement was profound to me. I realized that everything that I had achieved stemmed from the self-motivation I possessed and had learned to use throughout my life. For me, this self-motivation, what I now call the *D factor*, was learned from my father's example.

For most of us, our parents were our leadership role models just as we are the leadership role models for our children. In 1943, my father, Luther Cain, Jr., walked off the family farm in Tennessee and set out to find a job that would pay him a decent wage. He was determined to build a better life than that of his father, a small farmer who constantly struggled to survive. In Atlanta, my father had three jobs that he could work within a twenty-four-hour day. He worked as a barber, as a janitor at the Pillsbury Company, and as a chauffeur for the Coca-Cola Company.

My brother, mother, father, and I lived in a three-room duplex where the bathroom was outside on the back porch. My brother and I slept on a roll-away bed in the kitchen. Every day my brother and I quarreled over who would roll up our bed, a cot in the kitchen, and which one of us would roll out our bed at night. Then, on a bright summer Saturday afternoon in 1958, my father came home and told us to get in the car because we were going for a ride. We had no idea why Dad was home from work in the middle of the day or where we were going. He drove to a suburb west of Atlanta and pulled up in front of a small redbrick house and said, "This is our new home." I will never forget my father's proud moment of accomplishment. He was determined to buy our family a real house, and he did. Overwhelmed with happiness, my mother was in tears. My brother and I could not believe that our family could now live in a six-room house.

In many of my speeches, I tell my father's story not only because it demonstrates the D factor of leadership but also because it is a personal story that resonates with the audience. While not everyone experiences circumstances like mine, people do identify with life's challenges. They also want to learn from the example of others. No one likes to be told what to do, but they do want to be encouraged and inspired. People want to be led by someone who demonstrates sincerity and credibility through his or her relationships with family, neighbors, colleagues, and friends.

The Entrepreneurial Factor

Are you comfortable with risk? Are you prepared to be wrong, and will you accept the consequences of a wrong decision? Are you afraid of success or are you more afraid of failure? The answer to these questions is inherent in your risk index. If your index is 0.0, then you are totally afraid to live day to day. If your index is 1.0, then you are totally reckless. People who are successful as leaders and in life are somewhere between 0.5 and 1.0 because of the inherent risk associated with making decisions.

While it is a wonderful experience to establish new corporate profitability records and exceed personal goals, leaders must be able to manage the responsibilities that come with those successes and be accountable for their failures. Leaders who inspire others to follow them into new territory possess a high E factor, the entrepreneurial spirit. These entrepreneurs cast aside the forty-hour work week, leave the comfort zone of tenure and security, and charge across the perilous fields of change and opportunity. Continuous change is now the reality of our professional world. While we all try to work harder and smarter to stay ahead of the information revolution, leaders who possess a high E factor capitalize on uncertainty and use this energy to drive organizations forward.

Risk and leadership

These leaders are not reckless about the decision-making process. They use available research and insightful feedback from others. However, they do not wait for a "leadership moment" to make a decision, they make decisions when they are needed. The bottom line is that leaders with a high E factor are able to responsibly trust their gut instinct after all the analysis and evaluation has been done. There is really no such thing as a right or wrong decision, just different consequences for taking different actions. If the consequences are the desired results, then it was the "right" decision. A leader is perceived to be only as good as his or her last "right" decision. A speaker is only as good as his or her last speech.

The Focus Factor

Successful leaders block out the unnecessary and focus on the right problems. Think for a moment about the expression "You cannot see the forest for the trees." Most people have a natural tendency to be concerned only with the trees in their little corner of the forest, but leaders can instinctively maintain a perspective of the forest while being sensitive to individual trees. Clarity of focus is the key to the F factor. Just as a photographer can set a lens to highlight the primary subject in a picture while the other objects remain in the background, a leader is capable of focusing on the essence of a problem.

For example, I receive many invitations to speak about my experience as president of Godfather's Pizza, Inc. People have said they like my speech because Godfather's is a positive "turnaround story." Working with my management team from 1986 to 1988, we took the company from being a money-losing operation to one of the profitable subsidiaries of the Pillsbury Company. Ultimately, I participated in the leveraged buyout of Godfather's from Pillsbury, and Godfather's continues to prosper today. When people say Godfather's is a turnaround story, this is true, but we turned the situation around because we *focused* on the right problems. Godfather's had gotten into trouble earlier because it was trying to do too many things too fast and with too few resources. The essence of focus is doing fewer things well with the available resources. Leaders instinctively are able to achieve this balance.

ACT LIKE A LEADER

Leaders make things happen by removing barriers to self-motivation, obtaining results for the right problems, and inspiring people to exceed their expectations. Leaders must look, listen, learn, and then lead.

Remove Barriers

Since leaders cannot motivate people, as Drucker points out, leaders must then remove barriers that prevent self-motivation. The most challenging aspect of removing barriers for people, organizations, and even ourselves, is to identify the barriers in the first place. This is why it is so important for leaders to look, listen, and learn before they try to execute that leadership moment. For instance, at Godfather's Pizza, the biggest barrier to the company's success was its lack of focus. When I arrived at the company's Omaha headquarters in 1986, I picked up on several signs that the lack of focus was a major barrier for employees who wanted to succeed but were frustrated at every turn.

When the company had started to lose its competitiveness under the previous management teams, their strategy was to add variations to the menu. They reasoned that more menu items meant more choices, more choices meant more customers, and more customers meant more money. It had just the opposite effect. These new items created more operational complexity, which generated inconsistent execution, and product quality suffered. The most vivid example was the number of pizza crusts Godfather's offered—a thick crust, a stuffed piecrust, and an original crust, among others. Supposedly, this was to give the customers the ultimate choice of crusts and toppings made fast and fresh each time.

Without much consumer research, we discovered that what our loyal customers wanted most was a consistent original crust with their choice of ten different toppings made to order. So we eliminated the other crusts and concentrated on our original product, which allowed us also to execute better our training, operations, marketing, and advertising. The entire organization was then self-motivated to produce quality consistently, having identified and removed the biggest barrier to do so—too many crusts! Most people want to do a good job, but the job must be doable and they must be given the tools to do it. In this case, whatever created barriers to consistency needed to be removed.

My favorite family example of removing a barrier to encourage self-motivation is when our daughter, Melanie, went to college. My wife, my son, and I were very excited to see her when she came home after completing her first semester. We could not wait to hear about her experiences. As we sat down to enjoy dinner together, Melanie told us all about campus life and her classes. About midway through a delicious pork chop dinner that my wife had prepared, Melanie started to talk about an idea she had picked up from some of the other students. "You know, Dad, some kids are now taking five years to graduate." As we listened attentively, I said, "Is that right? Why is that?" Melanie went on to explain that kids in college nowadays (since her parents were obviously prehistoric) do not want to "stress themselves out." Melanie then stated, "I think I will take five years to graduate."

I stopped in mid-pork chop. With a fake smile on my face, I said to her, "Melanie, my darling daughter, my only daughter, my baby daughter. I want you to be happy, and if you want to take five years to graduate, that is your decision to make. But Dad is only paying for four years." By then I was not smiling. I did tell her, however, that I would pay for as many summer sessions as necessary within those four years. I, then, enjoyed the remainder of my pork chop dinner.

My darling daughter graduated in four years, right on schedule, which made us even more proud the day of her graduation ceremony. I am convinced that by removing a barrier, namely, Dad's money, that Melanie became self-motivated to graduate in four years. When our son, Vincent, started college six years later, Melanie was there to remind him that he would also only have four years to graduate. Tradition is a wonderful thing.

Focus in presenting ↗

When speaking in front of an audience, too many facts, figures, acronyms, charts, and examples that are not well organized will create a barrier of confusion for the audience. When people feel confused, they shut down. They lose focus on you as the speaker and on the heart of your message. Their minds begin to wander and they won't remember a thing you said. No one is inspired to change his or her opinion or behavior by someone who appears unprepared or overprepared. Speaking as a leader means that you are focused on removing barriers rather than creating barriers when it comes to communicating your message to the audience.

Obtain Results

I know this is a difficult notion for some people, but obtaining the right results starts with working on the right problem.

I'll never forget one of my conscious encounters with this commonsense notion when I changed careers to get into the restaurant business. Upon my successful completion of phase one in Burger King's restaurant manager training program, I was assigned my first head restaurant manager position. When my district manager met with me and made the assignment official and gave me my many marching orders, he simply said to increase the sales in the unit. This was after giving me a long list of things I could not do. For example, I could not change the price, the product, the advertising, or the promotion. In other words, he asked me to produce a sales increase with what I had inherited with the restaurant, and to do it in one quarter.

The following week, while managing the shift over a very busy lunch, I took some extra time to watch the customers' reactions as they received their orders and left the service counter. I noticed that the customers who had been greeted and served with a smile by one of the cashiers left the counter seemingly happier. So I wondered what would happen to sales if *all* the cashiers could serve the customers in that way.

One way to achieve that result would be to hire only cashiers who are what I call natural "beamers." You have experienced them yourself; people who can exude positive and happy energy to others seemingly without effort. Unfortunately, it is not possible to hire all natural beamers because there are not enough to go around. One day while I was working a register, I discovered something that I had not consciously realized before—namely, if you look a person in the eye and smile, it is almost impossible for them not to smile back—unless they are what I call the "walking dead."

The more I stressed to all the cashiers the importance of a warm and genuine service experience for our customers, the more nothing changed. I was working on the wrong problem. I believe it was Einstein who said, "Doing the same thing the same way and expecting a different result is insanity."

So I got the idea that maybe I could teach people, mostly teenagers in this case, how to "look people in the eye." To make it fun for the crew, I packaged this idea with three other fundamental points about providing great service and called it the BEAMer program, and those people who executed the four points most consistently were called BEAMers:

- *B*ad moods stay at home—I informed all crew members not to bring their bad moods to work. Surprisingly, most people complied, because it gave them an excuse to put aside their problems for a while.
- *E*ye contact with the customer—look them in the eye, look them in the eye, look them in the eye.
- *A*ttention on the customer—make sure they are happy the entire time they are in the restaurant.
- *M*ake every customer a happy customer—it begins with happy people.

To help communicate to the staff of the restaurant that I was serious, I had some buttons and T-shirts made for the crew to wear and hung a mirror in the back of the restaurant so the crew could do a last-minute BEAMer check before they took their position for the shift. I even got my district manager to let me pay for the materials out of my restaurant budget.

It worked! Within weeks, there were more smiles, more eye contact, more happy employees, and more happy customers who came back more often. After about three months of consistently promoting the BEAMer idea, sales were up significantly.

I had to identify the right problem and address it in order to obtain the right result—increased sales. Even my district manager was BEAMing.

Leaders must constantly ensure that the right problems are being worked on, and speakers must ensure that they are talking about the right things for that audience. Connecting with the audience with the right message and the right delivery is to *think before you speak.*

Inspire People to Succeed

Inspiring people with the spoken word is part gift, part learned experience, and part accident. The better you become as a speaker, the more good accidents you can make happen. Being able to inspire people (self-motivation plus passion) is to learn how to use the power of the spoken word to touch people. Saying the right words at the right time in the right way can truly touch people's hearts and souls. Just as the human body needs nourishment through food, the soul is nourished through words and other art forms, and the spoken word can be more powerful than the written word. Powerfully written words that are read by someone can change that person but not as far or as fast as those same words spoken effectively. Given the choice, would you rather have the words "I love you" given to you on a piece of paper or spoken to you by someone looking you in the eye. Let's hope that it is someone you want to hear this from!

Inspiring people to succeed begins with their having a dream or goal and believing it is achievable. Inspiration recharges their inner strength especially when the going gets tough or when they start to feel defeated. For example, this was the case with Jennifer, a student who heard my speech "Success Is a Journey and Not a Destination" at Johnson and Wales University. Jennifer had started to give up on a lot of things, when something I said helped her get back on track. When I met her by accident on the way to the auditorium, I had no idea things would turn out the way they did.

I was walking by myself on a beautiful sunny morning. As I passed this student, who was also walking alone, I said to her, "Are you going to the auditorium?" She said, "Yes." I asked her who was speaking and she said she did not remember his name. I then said to her, "Just another guy you have to listen to because it's a requirement for one of your classes." She said, "Yes." As we continued to walk and chat, she looked at me literally from head to toe and noticed that I did not look like a typical professor. I was sporting my usual corporate-blue-suit look. Suddenly, her expression turned from ho-hum to near shock and she almost stopped walking when she said, "Are you the speaker?" I answered "Yes" with a smile. At that point, she seemed like she was ready to crawl under the closest rock, so I said, "Don't worry, I used to have to listen to a lot of bad speakers when I was in college." By that time, we were at the auditorium and we introduced ourselves. I thanked her for the chat and went down to the front of the auditorium to meet my host and to get my lavaliere microphone.

The auditorium was filled with several hundred students as well as some faculty. I was introduced and then delivered my speech. The three key points in that speech are: Have a dream, say it out loud, and reach for your dreams one step (destination) at a time. I spoke for about forty-five minutes and received a standing ovation.

I gave the same speech again the following hour to another group of students, since the auditorium would not hold them all at once, and once again I received a standing ovation.

Following the second speech, I left the auditorium with my

host to attend a luncheon in my honor. As we walked out, Jennifer was waiting to intercept me. I was surprised to see her, since she had attended the first session.

She told me that she had heard my first speech and she wanted to tell me how much she learned from it. Obviously, I was extremely flattered. My host walked on ahead as Jennifer began to talk about how she had been touched by what I had said. She said she had been trying to decide what she should do after graduation. Because of some personal difficulties in her life, she was questioning her faith in God. As she began to get teary-eyed, I told her that the presence of hurt, disappointment, and pain she was experiencing at this moment did not mean that God had abandoned her, so she should not abandon God.

Something in my speech made a direct "hit" on her life. I believe it was the concept of success and life as a journey. I believe that after hearing how I overcame barriers in my story, she was encouraged to try to overcome hers. There is no message more powerful than a personal example; it adds credibility. Then, as we arrived at the luncheon site, she thanked me for listening and talking with her. I gave her my business card and told her to stay in touch. She did.

After Jennifer graduated, she wrote me a letter telling me that her "journey" was going well and that she was about to move on to her next "destination." She also shared that she was working on her long-term dream and that she had "said it out loud."

SPEAKING AS A LEADER— UP THE CORPORATE LADDER

When I was growing up in Atlanta, I did not know any keynote speakers. I did not know any corporate executives, and I certainly was not aware of the importance of developing effective speaking skills. My only frame of reference was the Baptist preachers I had heard at church on Sunday mornings. With their deep, booming voices, they conveyed tremendous passion for people and the importance of giving to others. Each week, I left church feeling invincible and ready to focus on the days ahead. Little did I know then that I would draw on these experiences for my own speeches.

In 1967, I graduated from Morehouse College with a degree in mathematics. My first professional job was as a mathematician with the Department of the Navy. Now, you are probably familiar with the boring, slightly geekish reputation of mathematicians. At least, this was the reputation of navy mathematicians at the time. When I was assigned my first presentation, I knew the audience had a preconceived notion of mathematicians and that the presentation would be a real challenge. One of my goals was to convey the information my audience needed to do their jobs more effectively; another goal was to show my audience that mathematics can be an exciting field. Since my job was to analyze the aerodynamic coefficients for various shipboard and aircraft weapons, bombs, and aircraft-fired missiles, these presentations were quite technical and detailed. Therefore, I developed a simple presentation strategy.

In the early days, I spoke from outlines. This required a good understanding of the material and a good deal of practice, but it also made it easier for the audience to follow my analysis and results. This was an important lesson about understanding the audience. A presentation or a speech is not about what you feel like saying at that moment. The goal is to recognize what information the audience wants to know and to deliver the message as simply as possible. An audience of technical analysts is very different from an audience of navy officers, and an audience of navy officers is very different from an audience of corporate executives. Mathematicians look for technical accuracy, navy officers look for target accuracy, and corporate executives look for a clear return on their investment of time. After six years with the navy, I earned a reputation for being a good speaker who could get to the point quickly and make mathematics interesting.

In 1973, I joined the Coca-Cola Company in Atlanta. This was my first corporate job, I do not recall *ever* giving a presentation where I was allowed more than thirty minutes in front of the audience. From this experience, I sharpened my "brevity with substance" skills. I practiced the Rule of Three: No more than *three* key points and no more than *three* key reasons for each of the key points. The underlying assumption, which I learned later, is that if I needed to bore them with all the details to make my points, they would not need me. As a speaker, you will lose your audience by giving too much information. In fact, communication research shows that we process only fifty percent of what we hear. In today's global environment, where we are so overloaded with information, it is *essential* to organize your information clearly and succinctly. Information overload is easy to do. Brevity with substance is an art.

Re: Brevity and information overload

In 1977, my early experiences with presentations at the Pillsbury Company were very similar to the experiences of my four years working at Coca-Cola. I managed a group of seven technical professionals, and was often required to present the results of my group's work to the operating executives. But the type of presentations started to change when I was promoted to director of information systems for the Consumer Products Division. I no longer had to make just technical presentations to upper managers, I also had to present to the one hundred people in my organization speeches on everything from corporate strategy to technology changes, and I had to explain the impact of acquisitions on their jobs and careers. Then I had to have them walk away feeling informed and inspired.

The business environment changed so quickly at Pillsbury that I had no choice but to trust my instincts when making decisions. When I allowed myself the freedom to make mistakes (the E factor), I was able to better focus my energy on truly leading a large organization. My former bosses and colleagues attribute my success to the fact that I asked the right questions and listened to what people said to me. I relied upon their experience and capabilities. My job was to make sure we were working together on the right problems in a timely manner. In essence, I became the *chief communicator*. My next assignment was to be in charge of a two-hundred-person information systems department as a result of Pillsbury's acquisition of the Green Giant Company.

Pillsbury's top business leaders were concerned about a computer processing disaster during the consolidation. Both organizations had approximately the same number of people and both had big computer systems. Each company had its own unique architecture. My challenge was to eliminate system redundancies and maintain the processing integrity required by the respective business units. We accomplished this goal without so much as a mild hiccup from these computer systems. Even though my graduate degree is in computer science, not once during the planning and execution of this tricky transition did I rely on my technical knowledge. It was my communications, organizational, and planning skills that were constantly being challenged.

A few months after the transition was officially completed, I was appointed vice president of corporate systems and services for Pillsbury. To say that my rise in the Pillsbury Company was meteoric is an understatement. In three years, I moved from manager of seven technical people to vice president for several hundred people. I am convinced, and this was confirmed by my bosses along the way, that this fast-paced advancement was accelerated because of my communications skills, which enhanced my apparent leadership ability.

When I resigned my vice presidency with Pillsbury in 1982 to start over at Burger King, my experience as an executive and a speaker did not start over. In fact, my previous experiences were key factors in moving from broiler person at Burger King to a vice president in nine months. During my nine months in "burger boot camp," my speaking skills were tested many times at the request of my district manager. Because the sales results in my restaurant were measurably and noticeably improved, I was asked to make several presentations at the district and even the regional level on creating happy customers. My district manager also asked me to help him prepare a presentation he had to make at a regional meeting. He admitted to me that he had no experience speaking in front of such a group. So, I gave him a crash course on "speaking as a leader," which helped him do a great job. To this day, whenever we see each other, he still reminds me of how those pointers helped him.

Following my nine-month fast-track training in restaurant operations with Burger King in Minneapolis, I finally received the big call from Burger King headquarters in Miami. I was selected to become the new vice president and general manager of the Philadelphia region. The region had performed poorly for several years, and my job was to "turn it around," as I had with my first restaurant manager assignment.

We did. This was achieved with the usual steps of focusing on operational basics, some organizational changes, and removing barriers that prevented people from being self-motivated to perform better and more consistently than they had previously. Many people refer to this last point as improving morale, which is the result of a group of self-motivated people becoming excited about what they can achieve together.

Most of the barriers that had to be removed were communication barriers among and between the various constituencies. Trying to apply the results of one restaurant to a region of four hundred and fifty restaurants was, indeed, a daunting communications and speaking challenge. This challenge was compounded by the fact that as vice president of the region I did not have total control over all the restaurants, since 350 of the 450 were franchised operations. My leadership and speaking skills were severely tested one-on-one, one-on-many, and one-on-everybody time after time.

Three and a half years later, the Philadelphia region had become one of the top performing regions of Burger King's ten regions in all categories. This was not accomplished easily since there were some constituencies within the region and in Burger King headquarters that wanted the region to succeed, but did not want Herman Cain to succeed. But results are just too difficult to ignore.

The chief executive of all restaurant concepts for the Pillsbury Company, Jeff Campbell, did not ignore the results of the Philadelphia region, which led to my becoming the new president of Godfather's Pizza in 1986. Godfather's Pizza had been acquired by Pillsbury as part of a larger acquisition several months earlier and was not expected to survive. My job was to "do it again, Sam!"

Two months after I first came to Godfather's Pizza as president, we had a companywide meeting of all operations and management people, franchise owners, and major suppliers of goods and services to the Godfather's Pizza system. The meeting was very well attended by nearly four hundred people, since everyone was curious about what "the new dude" was going to do to turn the company's performance around. Using an outline I had prepared on slides, I opened the meeting with a presentation of the new strategy. I did not talk from the podium, but instead, spoke from the floor of the meeting room using a lavaliere microphone. This created a much less formal feeling and more receptivity toward the "new dude" and projected a sense of confidence in the plan. I had also done my homework. I had done my homework because I had made my presentation before my key staff people several times to get their input and suggestions. My management team and I had developed a new strategy for the company with some new ideas and some old principles, which we introduced and discussed during the course of our day-long meeting. I then ended the meeting with a speech to the group entitled "Get on the Wagon" because I knew that not everyone there would enthusiastically accept this new style of leadership or the new strategy. In wanting to leave the message that we were not going to wait for those who were skeptical, I ended the speech with

> *Them that's going get on the wagon,*
> *Them that ain't get out of the way.*

Twelve years later, people who heard that speech still remind me of it, and that it was one of my best speeches ever, but, more important, they still remember the message of that speech.

Memorable Messages Enhance Focus

From the navy to Coca-Cola to Pillsbury to Burger King to Godfather's to the National Restaurant Association, and to my current position as CEO and President of Digital Restaurant Solutions, it has been an ongoing, never-ending learning process to create "the better speaker in me." How much speaking ability is natural I do not know, but I believe that we all have some natural speaking ability that can be maximized to create the better speaker in you.

Those early years of speechmaking, as I climbed the corporate ladder, provided valuable experience in developing the fundamentals of communications and speaking within the workplace environment. It wasn't until after I became president of Godfather's that I was invited to give my first keynote address at a major restaurant industry conference. That first keynote address was in 1988 in Los Angeles at the MUFSO (Multi-Unit Foodservice Operators) Conference of over fifteen hundred attendees. I had been asked to talk about the turnaround of Godfather's, which had received a lot of industry press attention.

I remember that they allotted me only twenty minutes because they did not know if I would be a good speaker or not. I also recall that my message that day consisted of two key points: The key to the turnaround of Godfather's Pizza was focus, and the biggest threat to our continued success was government.

After that speech, I was called the "pharaoh of focus" by *Nation's Restaurant News* magazine. I received dozens of requests to speak at other industry conferences and events, and I was invited to join the board of directors of the National Restaurant Association. I guess the speech went over pretty well.

This opened up a whole new dimension for me to grow as a speaker. Although there are a lot of similarities between speaking at conferences and speaking in the workplace, there are also some significant differences. First, when you are speaking to your team or group or department, they listen for their own self-interests. An audience listening to a keynote address does not necessarily have a compelling reason to listen and usually won't if you are a lousy speaker. Second, speaking to your team is usually on a subject of substance you select as the boss, whereas speaking to an outside group requires you to find some common ground on which to "connect" to the audience. Third, if you give an uninspiring talk to your people, they are not likely to express criticism or pass judgment on your delivery. A boring speech to an industry or outside group will result in a courtesy compliment and they will not invite you back or recommend you to anyone else.

Even with the similarities and differences, the fundamentals of a good workplace speech and an outside keynote are the same, namely: *Rule of Three* and *brevity with substance*.

CHAPTER 2

Message: Choose Your Words Carefully

"Words not only describe, they create."
—Archbishop Desmond Tutu

If you are familiar with Olympic swimming competitions, you will remember "Madame Butterfly." Representing the United States, Mary T. Meagher set her first record in the 200-meter butterfly in 1979 and became the third woman in swimming history to make three Olympic teams. With each powerful stroke, she showed the world her self-motivation, entrepreneurial spirit, and dedicated focus (the D, E, and F factors). Mary T.'s Olympic dream was by no means an "overnight success." She possessed talent and refined her skills through preparation and diligent practice in order to become a world champion.

When it comes to public speaking, your preparation process is much like learning how to swim. Visualize what it would be like if you dove into the deep water of a pool with no prior swimming lessons. You would splash around for a moment or two and then sink like a rock. However, if prior to your first dive you learned the fundamentals of swimming and could stay calm, you could plunge into a deep blue pool and have a chance at not drowning. Although few of us could win an Olympic gold medal no matter how long we practice, when it comes to public speaking, you *can* save yourself from drowning in front of an audience by learning several basic principles.

IT STARTS WITH AN INVITATION

Above all, remember that no professional organization would invite you unless someone believed that you would be a terrific speaker with a message for the audience. They hope that you will be inspirational but expect you to at least be informative. Moments after an invitation is accepted, however, some people lose sight of how their leadership skills prompted the invitation in the first place. For some reason, they allow their worst fears of personal rejection to turn an opportunity into a dreaded event. If speaking before an audience is a new experience or if you are an experienced speaker but still feel uneasy when the spotlight is on you, I suggest that you think about your E factor. Think about your tolerance for risk and ambiguity in relation to the event. Once you identify what is uncomfortable about the situation, you can then focus on removing the discomfort and capitalize on the opportunity. Here are some questions to ask in order to put the event in perspective.

1. Where did the referral come from? It is important to know who is singing your praises within the organization, your industry or community.
2. Ask specific questions about the event and the audience. Is this an annual meeting (monthly, quarterly, etc.) or a special occasion? Who spoke last year? What was the audience reaction?
3. Does the event have a theme? What topic do they want you to speak about?

4. Where are you on the agenda? Will you speak before or after a meal? Avoid speaking during a meal.
5. Will you have access to audiovisual equipment if you need it?
6. What are the time and place, and the estimated size and composition of the audience? Also, be sure to ask for the contact person and all appropriate contact information in order to follow up prior to your speech. Ask for all this in writing.

With this information in hand, the next step for you is to make note of as many related experiences as possible. You can organize, delete, or add later, but this starts the process of developing your message. Visualize yourself in front of the audience but do not be intimidated at the thought of the audience. Remember, you were asked to speak because they believe you have something in *your* experiences that the audience should hear. Then, as my grandfather used to say, "Sleep on it." Give your subconscious mind a crack at processing all your ideas before you try to structure your speech. By morning, or in a day or two, several good ideas for your speech will emerge in your mind.

FOCUS ON *YOUR* MESSAGE

How many speeches can you recall? What was the last speech you heard and what was the key message? Most of us have to scratch our brain to remember. Lack of speech recall simply means that you've listened to forgettable speeches by well-meaning speakers. This is a shame, because the spoken word is a powerful force. A great speech makes a connection with people and inspires them to think about something differently or change their lives in some way.

To make your speech a memorable one, focus on the *message*. What do you want the audience to remember, think, believe, feel, or walk away with from your speech? What do you want the audience to *focus* on as a result of your speech? As you draft your message, remember that the audience hears only fifty percent of what you say. Two days later, they will remember only half of what they heard. This is why a focused message is critical to your speech. For example, "Success Is a Journey and Not a Destination" is the title and key message of a speech I give about my climb up the corporate ladder, starting with my years growing up in Atlanta. I often give this speech at college graduations or business luncheons where young entrepreneurs are in the audience. Key points in the speech are:

- Have a dream
- Say your dream out loud
- Without a dream there is no journey

After I give this speech, people will often say to me that the message they heard was "The American dream is possible" or "It is possible to succeed if you believe in yourself." Both of these messages are embedded in this speech. People will also comment on how this speech caused them to restore the dreams they once had. Now, if this speech inspires only one person to become self-motivated to establish goals and dreams and to pursue them, the speech was well worth the effort. This is what the spoken word is meant to do. It is the leader's responsibility to choose words carefully and to use them effectively. When you are speaking, you are leading.

A GOOD STORY BRINGS OUT THE BEST IN YOUR SPEECH

People love stories. Stories make a message memorable, and, if it is a really good story, people might remember the point of your message. Stories create pictures and settings in the listeners' minds. They imagine themselves in the picture or think of someone they know who sounds like someone in the story. This creates an emotional connection with the audience. For example, I often use stories from my childhood to illustrate my belief in the power of dreams. One of my favorite stories is about my grandfather. He was a Georgia farmer all of his life, who would hitch a team of mules to the wagon on Saturdays for the weekly trip into town. The wagon was our means of transportation and the vehicle for taking the produce my grandfather had grown to the market. He had no patience for a young boy's procrastination on Saturday mornings. In his southern drawl he would call to everyone planning to go that day, "Them that's going— get on the wagon, them that ain't get out of the way!" When I use my grandfather's words and tell his story, people visualize him as a strong and respected character. They open their minds and hearts to the message—Do not allow anyone or anything to stand in the way of your goals. In the example of the Godfather's Pizza's strategy meeting, the audience did "get on the wagon." Twelve years later, the wagon continues to take us on an exciting journey.

In addition to stories, you can make your message memorable and illustrate your focus by using a poem, a famous quote, or a simple metaphor. There are many "inspirational hideouts" where you can find powerful and relevant thoughts to complement your message. Some of the hideouts I search most often are:

- A Scripture
- Words to a song
- A life-threatening experience
- An incident that happened that day
- One of my heroes
- A recent news story
- A scene from a popular movie
- A famous or not so famous quote
- A mistake from which I learned
- Something a family member often said

I use a story and a metaphor in my speech about how free enterprise is slowly being destroyed. The speech is entitled "Save the Frog." The story is about how a frog will stay in a pot of boiling water if you slowly add a little heat over a long period of time. Metaphorically, the frog represents free enterprise and the boiling water represents the "ations"—too much legislation, too much regulation, and way too much taxation. This metaphor vividly illustrates the gradual compounding of legislative, regulatory, and tax law on our system of free enterprise, which could eventually self-destruct from "boiling to death" if we do not reverse this trend.

Like many of you, I have seen poor speakers in action. What do they have in common? Poor speakers tend to talk too long, ramble aimlessly, or both. Under these circumstances, no one hears the message or cares. What's worse, the individual will never speak at another event. The word on the street, which travels quickly in today's high-tech world, will be that the person gave a terrible speech. In addition to being rude and unprofessional, it is unethical to come into a public speaking context unprepared. Busy people give a speaker their time, and they expect the speaker to have a worthwhile message. I'm not suggesting brevity over substance, but I am suggesting *substance with brevity*.

One of the best short speeches I ever gave was a three-minute acceptance speech for an award I received from Northwood University. It was at a black-tie dinner where several other people were also going to receive a business leadership award. The audience consisted of current recipients and their families and friends, past recipients with families and friends, students, faculty, and staff from the university. During dinner before the awards, all I could think about was how many of the same thank-you speeches this audience must have heard over the years. Since I knew that I had three minutes for my acceptance remarks, I thought of my Rule of Three and asked myself (while eating and talking during dinner) what three memorable points could I make from my heart. As I listened to the first two awardees preceding me, I decided on:

1. We were all put on earth to make a difference in the first place.
2. Our time on earth is a mere speck of eternity.
3. Life is just a minute.

My message was as follows.   *3:00*

Thank you very much, and in the three minutes I'm allowed, I'd like to make three points.

First of all, it is extremely humbling to be recognized for something that one considers an expectation of God almighty because I believe that we were all put here on this earth to make a difference, using whatever skills, talents, and abilities that God gave us.

Secondly, as I reflect upon my life and those things that I have been blessed to achieve, I am reminded of something that my grandmother reminded me of. She is one hundred and one years old and she lives outside Atlanta, Georgia. She reminded me that no matter how old you are or how long you live, your life is but a speck on that time line called eternity. And in that speck we have the obligation and the responsibility to make that difference that God put us here for.

And the third point that I'd like to leave you with I learned from Dr. Benjamin Elijah Mays, late president emeritus of Morehouse College, when he reminded us about the nature of that speck called life on this time line called eternity. He said, "Life is just a minute, only sixty seconds in it, forced upon you, can't refuse it, didn't seek it, didn't choose it, but it's up to you to use it, you must suffer if you lose it, give an account if you abuse it, just a tiny little minute, but eternity is in it."

Thank you for recognizing me during my minute.

Dr. Mays used the poem "Life Is Just a Minute" many times during my four years as a student at Morehouse. The students never tired of hearing it because we were inspired every time by his passion as he spoke. Since my graduation from Morehouse, now thirty-two years ago, I continue to use this poem because it is memorable and communicates a very powerful message for many situations. People who have never heard the poem often request copies, which I gladly send them. Dr. Mays continues to change people's lives through that poem.

THE ART AND SCIENCE OF MESSAGE DEVELOPMENT

Drawing on my experience in the restaurant industry, I like to say that messages are memorable when they are "shaped, shaken, and baked" in a way that will allow you to inform, engage, and inspire the audience. "Shaped" refers to what you are going to say, "shaken" is how you are going to say it, and "baked" is the process of fine tuning. You recall such great messages as: "A country pitted against itself cannot stand" (Abraham Lincoln); "Ask not what your country can do for you, ask what you can do for your country" (John F. Kennedy); and "I have a dream" (Dr. Martin Luther King, Jr.). These leaders spoke as leaders. Not only did they inspire people to change their lives; these messages shaped history and ultimately shaped the world.

The subconscious mind works hard to process information once the conscious mind relaxes its grip on the problem. This means that the conscious mind must forget about the barriers for a while by sleeping, playing a round of golf, listening to music, or anything that gets the conscious mind on something else. If the subconscious has enough information or facts, it will feed its findings back to the conscious mind when it is ready in the form of an answer or idea. I call this interactive relationship between the conscious and subconscious mind "shape, shake, and bake," which means write it, change it, sleep on it, and repeat the process until it feels good. You will notice that "shape, shake, and bake" is more memorable than "write, change, and sleep." As an example, my subconscious mind did not give me the ROI mnemonic that I now use in my "Leadership Is Common

Sense" speech until long after my book on the subject was published. The ROI concept (Remove barriers, Obtain results, Inspire others) germinated during each delivery of my leadership speech. After I hit the sixty-fifth performance, ROI hit me like a bolt of lightning.

Whenever possible, I spend time with the audience at one of their social functions or sit in on part of their program prior to my speech. Based on what I see and hear, I "shape" my speech by identifying examples and anecdotes relevant to the audience and determining how much time to spend on each key point. This technique works especially well for a speech given many times before, and it helps me to not get sick of listening to myself.

Allowing your subconscious to work (sleep on it) is also a good idea before you "shake," or rewrite your speech. This is especially helpful when developing a new speech or adding new material to an existing speech. But do not get carried away with the rewrites. Too many are like overmixing biscuit dough, which will produce heavy biscuits instead of light and fluffy ones. Several iterations between "shake and bake" (rewrite and sleep on it) may also help the speech or outline to become more compact, just as butter rises to the top in the churning process. Hot, fluffy biscuits with fresh butter are hard to beat. You need only add your favorite jelly, which in the speaking sense is practice, practice, and more practice.

INFORM, ENGAGE, AND INSPIRE THE AUDIENCE

When a speech *informs,* people learn something. It could be a historic fact about a subject, something useful for everyday life, or how you dealt with a problem. When speaking recently to an audience of restaurateurs from Canada, I wanted to add something Canadian in my speech to better connect them with my message. So, in order to drive home my message that "great leaders instinctively remove barriers to self-motivation," I talked about one of the most respected and well-known prime ministers of Canada, Pierre E. Trudeau. He was first elected in 1968, and one of his main goals during his sixteen years in office was to maintain a unified Canada. One of the biggest factors that threatened the breakup of Canada was the ongoing dispute about whether English or French should be the official national language. Trudeau removed that barrier by passing a law that recognized *both* languages as the official languages of Canada. So, the English and the French had to find something else to argue about. Even though the audience was obviously familiar with Mr. Trudeau and the language legislation, I described what they already knew in the context of a key leadership principle to illustrate the importance of "removing barriers." Some people would also call this speaking technique the repackaging of information, but they learned something *new* (removing barriers) in relation to something they already *knew* (the English vs. French debate). This is what I call the *"new-knew"* principle.

What you include in your speech to inform and drive home your message and key points is also a function of your interests, skills, talents, and personality. If you are not an archaeologist, then it may not be a good idea to use stories about rocks in your speech—unless you collect rocks or something related to rocks. Try to relate to things or experiences with which you have some firsthand experience that enhances your credibility.

In addition to personal experiences about my upbringing, relatives, and kids (who are no longer kids), I use analogies relating to math and science (since my college major was math with a minor in physics). One anecdote I like to relate is the bumblebee story. The bumblebee is not supposed to fly, according to normal mathematical and aerodynamic calculations, but the bumblebee does fly. He can fly because he was never told that he could not fly, so he *believes* he can fly. I use this analogy to drive home the importance of people believing in themselves. Achievement of anything by anyone begins with the belief that it can be done. The next time you see a bumblebee, just watch the power of believing. If you use a story, it is also important as to *how* you tell the story. A good story told poorly is like a good joke with a bad delivery. Practice to make it better.

When a speech *engages,* it grabs the attention of the audience and causes people to think. An engaging speech is a two-way intellectual and emotional collaboration between the speaker and the audience versus one-way entertaining by the speaker. An entertaining speech may cause the audience to laugh and wait for the next humorous line, but an engaging speech captures the audience in your thought process. That thought process is the path to your intended message. Stated another way, people can disengage most of their thought processes so they can relax or de-stress while being entertained, such as in listening to a symphony orchestra, watching a ballet, or hearing a comedian. An engaging speech involves the audience's thinking and emotions. By engaging the audience's thinking, a speaker establishes expectations that the audience hopes he or she fulfills.

Humor is a "condiment" to the speech. Humor should be used only if you are comfortable using it. Not everyone can deliver a punch line effectively. Something amusing about you or an editorial cartoon from a magazine or newspaper can be the safest tactic. The worst tactic is to tell a funny story and you're the only one laughing.

The opening proposition of my leadership speech is "Great leaders are born and good leaders are made." Making this bold statement establishes an expectation that the audience hopes I will explain during my speech. Another proposition in my leadership speech is the assertion that there are three critical characteristics of leadership (Think as a Leader) and three critical things a leader must do (Act like a Leader), which the audience expects me to identify as well as explain how I arrived at just "three plus three" factors.

Dr. Howard Thurman was known throughout the world as one of the greatest preachers of his day. I remember hearing him speak once, and he began his speech with "I'd like you to think with me for a few moments." An engaging speaker gets the audience to *think* with him or her and not just listen and laugh.

Remember that anyone can get an audience's attention by merely tripping on the way to the podium, but a good speaker engages the attention of the audience. A speech that is remembered only as being humorous will leave the speaker and the audience with a very empty feeling.

When a speech *inspires,* people feel something. This could be happiness because you said something that they wanted to hear or disappointment because you said something they did not want to hear. Words that inspire can touch a whole range of human emotions based not only on what you say but on *how* it is said. Inspiration in a speech that stirs emotions and feelings is more art than science because it must come across as being sincere. Speakers with natural charisma, celebrity status, or star power have a much easier time of stirring that "fire in the belly" with a speech. Most of us have to work a little harder to deliver a speech that inspires an audience. But if you believe in your message with all of your heart, mind, and soul, people will notice and they will want to learn more about you, your topic, and how they will be able to do more with their lives. This is what true inspiration is all about.

Telling stories of human triumph, success against the odds, good destroying evil, sacrifice instead of selfishness, winning versus losing, and the conquest of belief over disbelief is a good way to present inspirational nuggets within your speech. What works best for one person may not work best for another—be creative. As a speaker, you can't inspire the audience unless you truly believe in what you're saying.

Remember that inspiring words are food for the soul. And just as the body needs the right kind of food on a regular basis to function consistently, the soul needs regular inspiration to be consistently happy. Hope is the key to happiness, and inspiration gives people hope. Religious leaders and speakers use scriptures such as the Holy Bible, with its endless stories and words of inspiration. There is no such main source for the common everyday speaker like you and me. *I believe great speeches can be divinely inspired, but only a few can inspire divinely.*

So, when you receive that first "big" invitation to give a major speech, do not panic and try not to refuse it. Remember that it is important to accept as many "smaller" invitations to speak as practical for your schedule. More important, always make time to practice. Practice is the key to developing the better speaker within you.

Focusing on your intended message during message development will challenge your creative skills and at the same time help you to not worry about the imposing audience. As you master the concepts in this book, they will be like putty in your hands. And just as a good story will bring out the best in your speech, a good speech will bring out the best in you. A lot of people have good ideas and messages to share with others, but these ideas and messages are useless until they are transformed into a reality that is capable of helping people to be happier, more self-motivated, more focused or more capable of helping someone else.

Your life experience is the best source of fruitful and interesting ways to artistically develop a good message with the possibility of it being a great message. The audience reaction will let you know. When you inform, engage, and inspire an audience, you empower people. At that point, you are not just a speaker, you are a leader speaking as a leader. Choose your words and develop your messages carefully, because as Archbishop Desmond Tutu so appropriately observed, "Words not only describe, they create."

CHAPTER 3

Audience: It's Like a Date

*"Work hard, know when to keep your mouth shut,
and answer your mail."*
—THOMAS J. PENDERGAST,
ADVICE TO HARRY S TRUMAN, 1934

WHEN I AM INVITED TO SPEAK before an audience, I always look forward to the event. Each occasion is my chance to meet people, ask questions, and listen to their hopes, dreams, and concerns. People are generous with their time and attention, and I do my best to deliver a keynote address that will exceed their expectations. But every now and then, I find myself in a situation that tests my resolve and ability to focus under pressure. Every singer, actor, dancer, teacher, athlete, and coach has had his or her most terrifying experience at some point in their career. At these times, you feel you have no control over what is happening and you are tempted to just walk off, call it quits, leave the game, or throw in the towel. But one's inner resolve and competitive nature says to hang in there and make the most of a bad situation because it is far better than being a quitter. As an accomplished professional speaker, I, too, have had that terrifying experience. I call it "the speech from hell."

THE SPEECH FROM HELL

The invitation sounded good. The chairman had heard me speak on several other occasions and recommended to his board that I open their national meeting. The meeting was to be held in Anchorage, Alaska. I had been to Alaska prior to this invitation and looked forward to seeing it again. Anchorage sits at the base of the Chugach Mountains along the coast of Cook Inlet. It is as far north as Helsinki, Finland, and as west as Honolulu, Hawaii. Anchorage is known for its spectacular glaciers, some of which I had an opportunity to see on my earlier visit. I could not imagine a more majestic setting for a keynote speech.

As many of you know from experience, business travel can be tiresome, especially when you have to change planes. Anchorage is not easy to get to. From Omaha, Nebraska, I made three connections and spent most of the working day at an airport or on the plane. Upon my arrival, I looked around the gate area for someone from the association. Usually, an organization designates one of its members to meet the speaker and take him or her to the hotel. This is a common courtesy. For an instant, I thought I saw a driver holding a sign with my name, but no. Making the best of the situation, I gathered my briefcase and carry-on bag and queued up in the taxi line.

As the cabdriver drove to the hotel, I thought I would arrive to find a message or a registration package about the convention. At the front desk, I watched the clerk fumble around with the computer for several minutes. Fortunately, I did, at least, have a reservation at the hotel, but no messages. After a disappointing room service meal, I decided to go to bed early and to focus on the positive. Tired from traveling, I felt that this was my chance to get a good night's rest. I had hoped that in the morning, someone would contact me with the details of where and when I would speak and what time I would be needed for the sound check.

By noon the next day, I still had not heard from anyone with this well-known national association, so I inquired at the hotel if they knew where this convention was being held. The front-desk attendant directed me to the convention center. I was only a few blocks away, so I walked there and asked to see a convention program at the registration area. I figured that if I was not listed in the program, then maybe I had made a mistake about the date, time, city, or even the association.

I had not made a mistake. The program had me listed by name and photo as the opening keynote speaker for four-thirty P.M., so, I was at the right event. At this point, I was starting to feel uneasy. I had no idea what to expect next.

When I inquired as to where the auditorium was located, I found out it was across the street from the convention center. I walked over to try to do an impromptu sound check and to test my introductory video for that afternoon. I could gain access to the auditorium only by talking my way past a security guard. From his point of view, if I was the speaker, why did I not have an escort from the association? This was a fair question. I wondered the same thing. After I showed him my picture in the program, he let me through the door. I found the technical crew and told them who I was and what I needed to do. They kindly accommodated me after they finished what turned out to be a practice session for someone else on the program.

After a successful sound and video check, I walked back to the hotel to relax and then changed clothes for my presentation. I arrived back at the auditorium at four P.M. for what I thought was my four-thirty speech. When I arrived, one of the stagehands told me to wait in the speaker's ready room. At about four-fifteen someone from the association appeared in the doorway. "Mr. Cain," a woman who was thirty-something said as she smiled gleefully. "We are so pleased that you are our speaker. We've heard so many wonderful things about you. Is everything fine, how is the hotel?"

This woman had gotten on my last nerve and I had to restrain myself. "This is the worst hospitality I have ever received in my life,"

I told her. "But I do not want to discuss it now, because there is an audience of two thousand people who are waiting for me to address them at four-thirty P.M." I wanted to focus my thoughts and calm myself, because the audience could not care less about my experiences. More important, my reputation was at stake, so I had to put my anger aside.

With a shocked look on her face from my honest response, she informed me that someone would come to get me when it was time for me to speak. I simply said, "Thank you," and I was not smiling. As I said before, the program had indicated that I would be speaking at four-thirty P.M. I remained in the speaker's ready room drinking bottled water (no ice) and trying to remain calm. At four forty-five P.M. I decided to walk backstage, thinking that they might be running a few minutes behind.

When I got backstage, I discovered that there were a few other items on the program before me of which I was not aware. Specifically, a speech by the former governor of Alaska, a children's choir, a dancing moose, and a real live sled dog. I am not making this up! I was in total disbelief that this was happening until the sled-dog handler pushed past me to go onstage. Finally, I was introduced at five-forty P.M. I asked my host if he wanted me to give my forty-five-minute speech as planned, and he said, "Absolutely." At this point, however, I was not sure how a leadership speech would go over following the dancing moose, who was quite good, and the sled dog, but my "Hermanator" video pulled the audience back into a serious mind-set.

I was finally on stage at five forty-five P.M. According to the agenda, the gala cocktail reception had started fifteen minutes earlier. Most people had traveled that day to attend the convention. If their connections had been like mine, I knew that they would rather be at the reception than at the keynote address. It is always possible that there will be things beyond the speaker's control that could contribute to ruining the mind-set of the speech. Even the most polished and experienced speaker can experience a rush of communication apprehension—unproductive, worrisome thoughts that can undermine the speaker's concentration and confidence. The important thing is to pull yourself back into focus. So, that is exactly what I did. I focused and began my speech with as much enthusiasm as I could muster at the moment.

Fifteen minutes into my presentation, two video monitors at the edge of the stage started flashing "fifteen minutes." As I was in the middle of trying to deliver my speech and block out all previous distractions, I thought that message was flashed by mistake, since I had not asked to be reminded about how much time I had left. Five minutes later it flashed "ten minutes." I glanced to the side of the stage. Sure enough, my "hostess" signaled that I had to end in ten minutes.

Thinking that maybe the building was on fire, I went into the close of my speech. Fortunately, I had already delineated my DEF and ROI principles of leadership as I was about to get into a series of examples, my best stuff, illustrating these principles vividly and inspiringly. I still received a standing ovation, which simply meant I had disguised what was going on. When I got backstage, I asked the woman why I was told to shorten my speech. "Well," she said while trying to smile, obviously hoping I would understand, "the audience has to cross the street to the convention hall before six-thirty P.M. for the reception, or the police will not keep the street blocked off." Maybe I'm missing something, but I think two thousand adults, one moose, and a sled dog are more than capable of crossing the street without the police.

Since I wasn't invited to the cocktail reception, I walked back to my hotel and ordered room service for dinner. This was a repeat performance of the worst room service meal I'd ever had. What else should I have expected, I thought to myself as I tried to watch TV, "Was this payback for something I did as a child?"

The next morning someone else from the organization met me at six A.M. to drive me to the airport. To say I was happy to be leaving is an understatement. The person driving me to the airport had heard about my experiences the day before from the chairman who invited me. He wanted me to explain to him in detail what had happened, but I did not want to embarrass him in front of his wife, who had ridden with us to the airport. I checked in at the airport with my briefcase and a carry-on bag and headed to my gate. When I went through the security checkpoint, the guard asked to search my bag. He pulled out the souvenir gift that was given to all attendees. I had kept it, but I was unaware that it was a whaling knife, a real-life, genuine Eskimo whaling knife. The security officer informed me that it was considered a weapon and that I would have to go back to the counter, have them box it, and then check it to my final destination—or go to jail. I told the officer "Merry Christmas," that the knife was a gift from me to him, and proceeded on to my gate.

Once the plane reached cruising altitude, I began to relax. When I thought about those two thousand attendees who would be leaving two days later trying to get through security with their *gifts,* it was the first time I felt like smiling since landing in Anchorage the day before. In fact, I started laughing hysterically on the plane at the thought of all those people trying to get through security. The security guard probably opened up a whaling knife store.

Fortunately, most of my speaking engagements are not this stressful. Most of them have impeccable hospitality. But there is always the unforeseen in life. A successful speaker must be able to remain totally focused on the message, audience and delivery, *not* on being mad. Don't let the speaking context stress you out. Remind yourself that you have leadership qualities that put you in the position to speak in the first place. In my case, it was my gut instinct, part of the F factor, that allowed me to focus and eliminate the barriers of this stressful situation from my mind. Unchecked stress leads to speaking anxiety, and this will make a bad situation worse. As in leadership, focus is the key to becoming a powerful speaker.

Focus in leadership
and speaking.

A DATE WITH THE AUDIENCE

When preparing for a date with someone special, you want to look your best, feel your best, and be at your best. In order to be in your "best" mode, you try to know as much about the person as possible beforehand. You talk to mutual friends, you have watched him or her at a party, or you have been in a class together, a meeting together, or bumped into each other at an event. In each case, you get some instinctive sense about the person that makes you feel good about the upcoming date. When the date goes well, you become inspired and plan for the next date.

To give a speech without proper audience preparation is like going on a blind date. Only a few of them are successful. Getting to know your audience is to know yourself, the people, and the parameters. Giving a speech to an audience is something special, you want to be "at your best." When you are well prepared and at your best, you, too, can live through your own speech from hell.

Socrates said, "Know thyself." Allow your speaking style to be as natural as possible. Any speaking techniques you have learned from seminars or books should be adapted to you, not you to the techniques. You should adhere, however, to the basics of good posture, good English, eye contact with the audience, an occasional smile appropriately placed, and your hands and arms in free and relaxed positions during your speech.

Remember, it all starts with an invitation. Before you accept the invitation to speak before an audience, ask about the expected size of the audience, which influences the logistics of your presentation. Will you use an overhead projector with transparencies or will you use slides. More important, however, is that when you know the size of the audience, it is easier to prepare yourself mentally for your speech. Your goal is to minimize your stage fright. If you are expected to talk to an audience of two hundred and you walk into a room of two thousand, your brain might freak out and lock your lips, and then you can't talk. If it is two hundred instead of two thousand, your brain might not lock but your feelings might be hurt because eighteen hundred people did not want to hear you speak. If you have assumed the audience size without verification in the past, I trust you now know what "assumed" stands for in the business world. Don't make this mistake twice. Always confirm the number of expected attendees for your speech.

Because every audience is different, it is important to *know the people* who will be listening to you by developing a "sense" of their collective personality. As I have said, inspiring words are food for the soul. And just as your favorite sandwich or salad has texture and flavor, speeches have context and tone. The method you use to deliver your speech depends on the information and the personality of the audience. The message could be a formal address about company performance or a keynote speech focused on a motivational topic. For the former, it may be appropriate to have a scripted speech if you are presenting detailed financial or operational information; for the latter, an extemporaneous style lends itself to motivational themes.

I use several ways to get to *know the people* in the audience, so I can connect during my speech. Reading the program booklet beforehand, attending a social function or dinner the evening before a speech, reading one of their newsletters, or sitting in on part of their meeting program are all great ways to get to *know the people*. Listening to other speakers on the program and the audience's reaction is by far the most effective way to develop that sense of the audience. Occasionally, I get a chance to listen to another outside speaker who precedes me. Since audiences react differently to outside versus inside speakers (one of the members of their group), being able to listen to another outside speaker before me is like a lay-up shot in basketball. I can hear their style, humor, and content while watching the audience's reaction from the back of the room. And if a previous speaker makes a point particularly relevant to what I will be presenting, I make a mental note and refer to it, if appropriate, during my speech. Having a "feel" for the personality of the audience helps me to understand different reactions to the same humor and to adjust key points and the tempo of my delivery. Find those common denominators between you and the audience and even other speakers on the program, and then draw on your personal experiences.

The better you *know the people,* the better you will be able to select stories, examples, or personal experiences that will help you connect to the audience. I can generally connect and relate to almost any age group and any type of audience. But I have repeatedly turned down requests to keynote at a morticians' convention. I have a hard time imagining what they would consider humorous.

Knowing yourself and getting to know the personality of the audience are most directly under your control. You just do it based on the time and opportunities available to make the necessary assessments. On the other hand, the parameters of the situation surrounding your speech are less under your direct control and can ruin a speech much faster than not knowing the audience, because there are so many variables that can affect the outcome. You can minimize the variables by testing them ahead of time, so when they say lights, camera, action, you are ready to go.

LIGHTS, CAMERA, ACTION

Before movie directors begin to shoot a scene, they make sure that all the technical parameters are ready before they issue the famous phrase "lights, camera, action." After your introduction as the speaker, it is too late to even think about the parameters. I learn as much as I can about the technical setup and parameters of the event *before* they say "Ladies and gentlemen, please welcome Mr. Herman Cain." I do this in order to minimize distractions during my speech. Type of speech, length of speech, room setup, audio capabilities, lighting, staging, size of audience, and program changes are all potential distractions if you do not know them in advance. Breakfast speeches, luncheon speeches, dinner speeches, keynotes, breakout sessions, panel discussions, acceptance speeches, and remarks require different preparation because they will have different expectations by the audience and differing amounts of time—sixty minutes, thirty minutes, twenty minutes, ten minutes, or even three minutes. So, go check them out ahead of time.

Technology can be daunting, especially when all eyes are glued on you. Podium microphone, cordless handheld mike, lavaliere mike, or no mike at all can throw off your concentration if something unexpected occurs during your speech. Be aware that the most annoying and unprofessional thing to do is to tap on the mike after you are introduced to hear if it's on, or, worse yet, blow into the microphone. All of this should be done ahead of time. If it is not possible, approach the microphone as if all systems are go. If there is a problem, take control and ask the sound manager to adjust the equipment immediately. For speeches of thirty minutes or less, a podium mike is fine, but for longer speeches, you may want to consider another option as well as some visual aids unless you are extremely interesting, animated, or you are just wonderful to stare at for long periods of time.

Although it may seem obvious, and it should be by this point in the book: Know what topic you are expected to talk about. The worst distraction is being introduced as speaking about a topic that is not the one you expected. I was about to give a keynote address to a large group of direct marketing and salespeople. When I accepted the engagement through my speakers' bureau, the client had asked me to speak on one of my topics, "Leadership Is Common Sense." As I was being introduced, the announcer said, "Ladies and gentlemen, and now to speak on 'Success Is a Journey' is Herman Cain." I was shocked!

I give keynotes using a memorized outline, without a written script, without notes, without a podium, and with a lavaliere microphone. I consider myself to be naturally animated and I like to eliminate as many physical barriers between myself and the audience as possible. I usually develop my outline the night before, after I get to know the audience and other speakers (watch and listen) a bit. I had not been informed of the switch in topics, and I had not received a copy of the final printed program, or I might have caught this ahead of time. Fortunately, they had to show my three-and-a-half minute "Hermanator" video before I started my speech. So, I had three and a half precious minutes to refocus my thoughts. The speech was extremely successful, but that momentary shock is not something I want to experience very often. So, I will say again for the record, it is very important to double-check the topic ahead of time. But if you do find yourself in such a situation, never apologize profusely to the audience for the mix-up. They do not care. Secondly, if you cannot switch topics that fast, then shorten your remarks to a few key observations and then orchestrate a longer question and answer session, if appropriate. But never bring the mix-up to the audience's attention unless there is a compelling reason to do so. Be professional.

If the audio/visual crew is setting up only fifteen minutes before the program is supposed to start, you could have a problem. This happened to me early in my keynote career. I had arrived one hour earlier than the scheduled speech, and the audiovisual equipment was not set up. For this speech, I was using slides, and I stood behind the podium and talked from the outline as the slides advanced. Since he was behind schedule, the chief audiovisual person said, "I'll take care of your slides. I am a professional and I do this all the time." I gave him my slides, asking if I could advance them from the podium. He said, "Yes, the clicker is on the podium."

Well, the clicker was on the podium, and as I started to advance my slides during my presentation, I noticed the slides were out of order and, as an added touch, several of them were even upside down. My brain did freak out. I tried to keep going, but there were too many slides out of order and upside down. I took control of the situation and asked the projectionist to turn off the machine. I talked extemporaneously for the rest of my speech using my outline from memory. The audience seemed pleased with the presentation despite the handicap. Afterward, I asked the man what happened, and he admitted he dropped my slides while loading them in the slide tray.

When circumstances happen beyond your control, my general rule is to go with the flow rather than fight the distraction. Fighting the distraction only brings more attention to it. Recently, I gave a speech to an audience of over two thousand meeting planners. In the middle of my speech, a lady's cellular phone started ringing and she could not stop it. So, I kept repeating myself every time it would ring, which amused the audience. Finally, she got up and left the auditorium. When she got outside to the foyer, the audience and I could still hear it ringing, so I continued the antic of repeating myself. Finally, it stopped, and after about a minute, the lady returned to her seat. I interrupted my speech to ask her, "Are you supposed to bring a loaf of bread or a quart of milk home?" The audience laughed and appreciated my patience, and so did the lady. Go with the flow when the unexpected happens.

Another distraction occurred during a speech I gave on March 24, 1998. It was a two-thirty P.M. "freenote" speech in a nice auditorium with about three hundred restaurant people to whom I enjoy speaking because of my natural connection to the hospitality industry. Usually, the "Hermantor" introduction tape plays a captivating opening by Herman Cain, but not this time.

During the playing of the three-and-a-half minute intro videotape, I noticed a sound distortion in one of the house speakers. Once again, the audiovisual people were not ready in time for a sound check. The distortion persisted throughout and was also evident earlier during the personal introduction of Herman Cain. Thinking that the distortion would not be in my lavaliere microphone, I began speaking, only to discover that the distortion was throughout all the microphones. The distortion was a big distraction to me in trying to follow my train of thought, and I could tell that it was also a distraction to the audience, because they kept looking at the ceiling and at one another.

The auditorium had a seating capacity of about four hundred people, which was small enough to speak without a microphone *if* you have a strong voice capable of projecting without hurting yourself. So, I removed the microphone, put it aside, cranked up my bass-baritone vocal cords and spoke loud enough for the last row to hear me. The audience applauded because the distortion was annoying to them as well.

Unexpected distractions can come from anywhere, but the more you eliminate known possible distractions, the easier it is for your brain to stay focused on its mission of calmly controlling the voice, the eyes, and the body language. The delivery of your speech actually begins before you speak; it begins the minute you walk into the room. If you have done your homework and prepared properly, you will feel confident and look confident to your eager listeners. And unless something drastic happens, stick with your game plan.

DISTRACTIONS IN THE AUDIENCE

There will be times when distractions cannot be anticipated or avoided. Leaders know instinctively that every work group, organization, and public situation is going to be a unique experience. Just as you must prepare for the occasional dancing moose prior to your turn at the podium, you must prepare for unexpected distractions. To prepare for unexpected distractions, simply keep the possibility in the back of your mind that if they do happen, you will not get off focus and lose your train of thought. Worse yet, distractions can cause you to get into a negative mood during your speech, which could then come through to the audience. Always leave the audience on a positive note, because someone might be on the brink of giving up and a negative ending might push them over the edge.

Other than the nightmare in Alaska, I have experienced more and more baby and cell phone distractions lately. A couple of years ago, a toddler of about three years with a red balloon was sitting in her mother's lap in the front row of the audience—not the back row, but row one, almost dead center. The balloon was on a string and the child was playing with it by making it go up and down. I tried to ignore it, but the audience would look over at the toddler every time the balloon would go up and when she giggled. A woman who appeared to be the child's grandmother got up to take the child and the balloon out. I thought it was over and I could continue uninterrupted. But ten minutes later, they returned, and the grandmother even let the toddler run down the side aisle across the front to where the child's mother was sitting.

I must admit that I had a difficult time not letting my annoyance show, but I held it back. Fortunately, I was near the end of my speech by that time, and rather than continue to compete with the little girl and the balloon, I cut about ten minutes off what is usually a fifty-minute blockbuster speech. I decided to shorten the speech as the way to handle the distraction because the audience could not block it out even though I could. To my surprise, the parents with the child and the balloon and the grandmother approached me following the speech to tell me how much they really enjoyed the talk.

I had another incident involving another baby in the audience during a black-tie event. In this case, I had created a captivating mood during the speech when, suddenly, the audience and I could hear a baby starting to get fussy. This was no three-year-old; it sounded more like an infant. Although the distraction from the baby broke the captivating mood, I ignored the sounds and continued as planned, and the speech was successful. When distractions come from babies or kids, I usually try to ignore them because the audience is already wondering why the parents do not take control of the situation by taking the child outside the room. The speaker does not have to further embarrass the parents.

Nowadays more and more people have cell phones, and they will leave them on or forget to turn them off. In either case, it is rude to the audience and the speaker. If I hear a cell phone ring while I am speaking, I will make an impromptu humorous remark depending on where I am in the speech. I may even choose to ignore it unless it persists. What you do will depend upon the situation and how comfortable you are with a noninsulting, quick-witted comment. Some of the more successful comments I have used to leverage the cell phone distraction are "Did he want you to bring home bread, milk, or beer?" "Tell them I'm busy right now, thank you," or "Is it Elvis?" When in doubt, just ignore the ringing cell phone and the audience will give the person some withering looks or transmit to them some scolding thoughts, which are thoughts you know the audience is thinking, such as "How rude" or "You idiot!"

If the speaking occasion allows for a question-and-answer period, the people asking the questions can also be a form of distraction. If the question is directly relevant to your message, then there's no problem. But if you get one of the other popular types of questions, they can leave your audience confused and removed from your message. The most common types are:

a. The illegitimate question. This question does not relate at all to your speech. It is intended to test you and to throw you off track. The person asking the question is trying to sound thoughtfully provocative for his or her own gratification. In these situations, I often respond with "I have no idea what you are talking about, next question."

b. The nonquestion. This is a mini speech by someone who wants to use your podium to give a speech of their own since they have not been asked to speak anywhere recently, if ever. After this individual has gone longer than a simple question should take without clearly asking a question, I sometimes respond with "Would you repeat the question," which I use if I know the person, because it could embarrass them. Most of the time, I respond by saying, "You raise an interesting point and I don't have a counterpoint right now." Most of the audience will know it was a nonquestion.

c. The grenade. This is the antagonist who is trying to discredit or embarrass you. The so-called question may be in the form of an accusation against you without any evidence or support. For example, I did a live radio program (a continuous Q&A) where someone called in and accused me of stealing from my employees only because he had just read an article about a CEO who had made a big bonus. I simply said, "I resent your accusation of me based on an article you read about someone else, could we please move on to a legitimate question?" Whenever you are faced with a grenade, I recommend that you take the high road and not get into a ridiculous debate that could make you sound unnecessarily defensive. This is what the grenade thrower wants. Do not give such a person the satisfaction.

Most distractions during a speech are unexpected, and the best way to handle them will be dictated by the circumstances. As a general rule for handling distraction, you can:

- Ignore the distraction.
- Acknowledge the distraction by stopping until it ceases.
- Make light of the distraction if you can think of a quick-witted comment, but try not to be insulting because that's the "low road."

Whatever the distraction, don't let it control you or your message.

THERE IS NO SUCH THING ✳✳
AS OFF THE RECORD

There are two golden rules about confidential information. One, the only way to keep something confidential is not to tell anyone. Two, if you tell someone a piece of confidential information, they will tell someone else. It's just a matter of when and how. It is human nature.

Some organizational cultures are worse than others. Similarly, some people are worse than others at keeping confidential information because they believe it is their job to tell the world. For some people, keeping a secret is like having a grenade inside of them that is on an automatic timer and will explode if they do not release the pressure by telling someone. And if a person is in the news reporting business, then they are on automatic release. Because as they would tell you, it's their job.

There are obviously exceptions to these rules. And reporters who are able to keep things off the record are really saying they will identify you only as an "unknown source" when they report on the fact, rumor, or information. But such exceptions need encouragement. Threatening to never give them another interview or story or hot tip usually works because that's like cutting off their blood supply. Remember, it's their job.

When speaking to an audience composed mostly of people you do not know, how long do you think everybody in the room will keep something you said confidential? Not long. Additionally, what you said will change as it spreads like a "big fish that got away" story. Recall the game you played as a kid called post office. When I was in sixth grade, the teacher would sometimes let the whole class of thirty-five kids play giant post office. The first kid would whisper a message to the next kid and proceed successively until the message got to the last kid, who would repeat what they were told out loud. The rule during the game was that you could whisper to the kid next to you only once. Invariably, the message at the thirty-fifth kid was totally different from what it started out to be. If you do not want to be the focus of the "big laugh," I suggest that you think carefully before you speak and heed the advice of Thomas J. Pendergast to Harry S Truman: "Know when to keep your mouth shut."

The post office game taught me two very valuable lessons—listen carefully and be careful what you say and how you say it. When information leaves your lips, it is on the information superhighway, capable of picking up "passengers" along the way. In my introductory biography, for example, which is routinely used by host organizations to prepare pre-meeting promotional materials and the actual intro-duction for the event, it clearly states that I "worked for the Depart-ment of the Navy" early in my career. At least three out of ten times I am introduced as having "served his country valiantly in the navy."

The key message here is not to be paranoid about every word or innuendo in your speech, because that would restrict your cre-ativity and speech delivery. However, sensitive information should be omitted or treated delicately because there really is no such thing as off the record.

CONNECT AND CAPTIVATE

Even though people may relate to your subject matter or topic or message, they also want to *connect* to you as a person based on some-thing that *illustrates* that you are a person just like they are. In many of my speeches, I relate an experience that illustrates (not just pontificates) my humble beginnings as the son of a domestic worker and a chauffeur. I talk about my experience of making a career change, or the experiences of raising my children. I relate my expe-riences in the real world of restaurant operations and the real world of having to fire people with compassion so they could get on with their lives. Use personal stories and examples to illustrate your mes-

Re: Motivational Speaking)

sage and key points, or use stories to which the audience can relate.

Similarities and common denominators can be personal or they can stem from business backgrounds, beliefs, frustrations, experiences, hard times, dreams, interests, values, problems, pet peeves, disappointments, or victories. The possibilities are endless. Not everyone will connect, but most people will if your message is clear and you know your audience. As you will read in Chapter Four, most people will like *something* on your "sandwich."

When I speak to restaurant unit level operators, I use true stories of when I was running a Burger King. I often tell the story of how I taught my front counter servers (mostly teens) to smile genuinely when assisting customers. This is the BEAMer program I noted earlier. Now I will tell you the rest of the story.

One day a customer stopped me and asked if I was the manager. I indicated yes, and she proceeded to tell me that she came in on a regular basis. She then asked, "How did you get all those teenagers to smile at the front counter?" I thanked her and explained the BEAMer program. As a result of the program, the restaurant's sales increased twenty percent over trend by executing the basics and making people feel genuinely welcome by looking them in the eye. You obviously cannot look every person in the audience in the eye, but you can look selected people in the eye. This will make the whole audience feel a sense of eye-to-eye contact. It also projects an air of confidence, which helps to capture their attention.

When talking to business executives, I relate instances of success and failure or instances of having to perform difficult terminations. I can recall twice in my career when I have had to fire someone (redirect their career) because they were simply in the wrong job and the wrong profession. In both instances, I let them go with compassion and dignity, and in both instances, they later called me and thanked me for firing them. This had forced them to find a profession they were much happier doing day to day. Dismissing anyone from a job is stressful, and no one enjoys the task, but an audience connects immediately with describing how a difficult dismissal handled properly can have a long-term happy ending.

When addressing a general audience, personal and family experiences work well, especially if they are humorous. Humor about yourself helps people to see you as a "regular" person, which connects them to you.

You can also connect to an audience by trying their product, if possible, before you speak and relate the experience and perceptions. If it was a bad experience, don't bring it up. If it was a good experience, use it where appropriate. I did this recently in Orlando, Florida, on my way to a general manager's conference for a retail merchandise company. I had never been in one of their stores, so I had the limo driver stop at one on the way to the speech. It was a great experience. In fact, I had a button missing from one of my shirtsleeves and wanted to test their reaction to a simple yet uncommon request. When I entered the store, I looked around for a few minutes, then found the men's department. I explained my situation and asked if they could find a button and sew it on for me. They said with a smile, "No problem," and I'm sure they did not know where I was headed. The lady who actually sewed the button on did so without my having to take my shirt off. I was already dressed for the speech I would be giving that afternoon.

I incorporated the incident into my speech as I talked about achieving exceptional service. They absolutely loved it! I think I connected with this audience for life using this true experience. A week later, I ran into the CEO of this company in a restaurant in Washington, D.C., and when he saw me, he insisted on introducing me to his guests. He then began to extol about how great my speech was and how they now have a new company motto, namely, "Make every button count."

When speaking to the general public, such as at a community function or organization special event, I try to share perspectives on

issues and events that are topical and current. For example, following
the 1999 tragedy at Columbine High School in Littleton, Colorado,
I opened a speech with reference to the incident and asked what
went wrong that could cause those two boys to kill others and then
kill themselves. I then said I believe they did what they did because
they were not happy, because happiness is

Something to love,
Something to do, and
Something to hope for.

Those two boys had no hope, and therefore their lives and the
lives of others had no significance to them. This unfortunate incident
connected with the audience because hardly anyone could have
missed hearing about this tragedy.

I can always depend on government bureaucrats or politicians
to provide something topical. Just read a newspaper or listen to a
news program to determine something that might connect in your
speech. For example, when the Federal Aviation Administration
issued a regulation that airlines had to create "peanut-free zones" on
commercial airplanes for the minuscule percentage of people who
are allergic to peanuts, I used this as an illustration of how our government has gone too far with too much regulation. With all due
respect to people who are allergic to peanuts, there are probably
more people allergic to shrimp and other shellfish. Does the FAA
need to also create "shrimp-free zones," and then "dust-free zones,"
or how about "milk-free zones," "tomato-free zones," and so forth.
Eventually, the entire airplane would be empty if some common
sense is not used. Incidentally, I am allergic to idiots, so I should have
the right to sit in an "idiot-free zone." The audience can connect to
this FAA regulation because most of them had heard of similar absur-
dities in government.

Connecting to your audience at your staff meeting is inherent—you are the boss. However, boss authority does not equal leadership. Just as you need to know your audience, you need to know the people in your organization. They must be self-motivated to perform well and to deliver the results you expect from them. You must look, ask questions, listen, remove the barriers to success, and inspire them through your words and deeds.

Connecting to people can sometimes occur on points you least expect. After having spoken professionally for several years, I was approached by someone who said they "connected" to me on something that no one had ever mentioned before. Of all the things I related in the speech that day, this particular gentleman told me that his father was also a barber.

I often tell the story of how my dad worked three jobs, one of which was as a barber, but this was the first time someone felt so connected to me on that point, and he mentioned it several times over the course of the next several hours. He was as proud to be a barber's son as I was, which was his connection to me.

When each person in an audience feels that you have walked in their shoes in some way, they accept your message with greater credibility. You might even change someone's life.

Captivating an audience's attention means to *get* and *keep* their undivided attention. As I have said before, if you fall down on the way to the stage, you will get their attention, but falling down for thirty minutes will not keep their attention. Have you ever noticed how some speakers get the audience's attention with a joke or humorous story but lose them right after the laughter? Or, have you noticed the speakers who begin with all the formalities of thanking everybody in the room and the world for inviting them to speak? It's their way of saying that if they give a lousy speech, it's everybody else's fault. There are times when giving appropriate thanks is required as a matter of courtesy, but it can be accomplished quickly, or during your speech.

The biggest mistake in getting the attention of any audience is

Getting an audience's attention

assuming that you already have it simply because it's your time at the microphone. Speakers who have star power usually get immediate attention or they can get an audience's attention with a pregnant pause—a few seconds of only eye contact with the audience before a word is spoken. Johnny Carson is a master of the pregnant pause. But for most of us, it's not that easy, so practice the technique. Also, you should make a point of being attentive to how other speakers use the pregnant pause. The more you look, listen, and learn from others, the more productive your practice sessions will be for you.

I have used several techniques to get an audience's attention since I speak so frequently in so many different situations. My favorite opening technique is to recite (without notes) a poem or a famous quotation that usually relates to the message I plan to deliver. Over the years, I have developed a repertoire of poems and quotations from which I select to use as an attention-getter. For impact, I recite them from memory so I can "look the audience in the eye" while I talk. It is a very effective technique, but it requires a lot of practice. If you are serious about advancing in your career as a leader in your organization or industry, these techniques are well worth the investment of time.

When I started speaking professionally (i.e., getting paid!), I wanted to distinguish myself from other speakers, so I created an introductory video that highlights sound bites from several speeches I had given over the years. This is particularly useful when you are not sure whom or what you might follow in the program such as a dancing moose or sled dog. The video refocuses them on me, who I am, and a sampling of my messages and style. I would still use a poem following the video to lead into my speech, but the video sets "my stage."

One of the most captivating openings to a speech I have ever read was given by Lea Rabin in a speech at Harvard's John F. Kennedy School of Government. She is the widow of the former prime minister of Israel who was assassinated on November 4, 1995.

She was with him when he was shot. Her account of the incident is so riveting, one can almost hear her speaking these words:

I want to thank President and Mrs. Rudenstine, Dean Joseph Nye of the Kennedy School, and Heather Campion, director of the Forum, faculty, students, friends who are here tonight. I have spent the day, a very stormy, snowy day here in Harvard, and I can only say how very impressed I was with all that I sensed and saw, and it's a great inspiration to be here with you tonight.

On November fourth, at eleven-fifteen P.M., it was announced to the world media, the prime minister and minister of defense, Yitzhak Rabin, is dead. He was shot by bullets coming down the stairs after the peace rally. We, myself, our children, Mr. Perez, Mr. Weitzman, other members of the government, and many, many friends were in the room in the hospital, knowing already there was little hope to save his life, expecting the worst. Yitzhak Rabin is dead. We went to kiss him the last time and left the hospital.

Just two hours before, you could see him on the platform in front of the two hundred thousand who were there for the first time after a long period of silence, singing, dancing, and yelling. We want peace. Rabin, Perez. We love you. Rabin, Rabin. Yitzhak could hardly believe this sight, this joy, this love pouring at him, at the peace. He was a happy man. He said yes to peace, no to violence. And he sang the song of peace. He worked hard and loved. He hugged and loved and played. Rabin, Rabin, we love you. Lea, take good care of him. And I said, I've tried my best. Last word before I heard the bullets, saw him falling, and did not yet believe he was even hurt. This sight will forever stay with me, like you stop the video on a certain point, and there it is forever. I did not know, but he was shot and clinically dead a few seconds later in the car.

No one wishes such a tragic loss on anyone, and it certainly takes a very strong person to be able to recount such an event in such detail. I am personally inspired by her courage and her continued advocacy for the principles of peace that Prime Minister Yitzhak Rabin lived and died for.

I had the honor of meeting Mrs. Rabin in Amsterdam at a meeting of the International Hotel and Restaurant Association in 1997. I was the keynote speaker for the program and she was presented the association's first annual International Peace Award in honor of her late husband.

From this chapter I hope you have learned that getting the audience's attention can be achieved effectively in a relatively short time span, namely, the beginning of your speech. *Keeping their attention,* which is a bigger challenge, is a function of your total message. Let's move on to delivering your best stuff to the audience.

CHAPTER 4

Delivery: It's Not a Pizza

"Speeches measured by the hour die with the hour."
—THOMAS JEFFERSON

THOMAS JEFFERSON'S INSIGHT about public speaking remains true. Reading pages of text to an audience is not a speech—it's boring! Great speeches inform, engage, and inspire people. When a speech informs, people learn something. When a speech is engaging, the language flows and takes the audience through a thought process that allows them to visualize your message. A great speech captivates the attention, the minds, and the hearts of people. When people's hearts are touched, they feel inspired.

DELIVERY—IT'S A SANDWICH!

Now, I know the analogy I am about to make may seem like a stretch at first, but trust me for a moment. The process for giving a speech is like the process of building a sandwich. You start with the choice of meat (message), then select the type of bread (opening and closing), and then the condiments (stories, facts, examples) you want on your sandwich, then you serve it (delivery) on fine china or paper plates. A sandwich is not just a sandwich when it is customized and served with style.

For example, when I am asked to speak before a group of executives, the topic usually has some connection to leadership. My "Leadership Is Common Sense" speech opens with portions of Rudyard Kipling's poem "If." "If" is one of my favorites because Kipling's words inspire one to dream, and he challenges the reader to become the leader of his or her own destiny.

> *If you can dream and not make dreams your master,*
> *If you can think and not make thought your aim,*
> *If you can meet with triumph and disaster and treat those*
> *two impostors the same,*
> *If you can fill life's unforgiving minute with sixty seconds of distance run,*
> *Yours is the earth and all that's in it,*
> *But even more you'll be a [leader].*

The "meat" of the speech consists of the three plus three principles of leadership—D, E, and F factors *plus* ROI factors. For the condiments on this sandwich, I select from my experiences. One of them is the challenge I faced when I became president of Godfather's Pizza, Inc. I also use stories, anecdotes, or other people's experiences to drive home the key message. And then I close with "Life Is Just a Minute," "The Tragedy of Life," or another poem, depending upon how I shape the speech and my sense of the audience.

If you stop and think about it, the audience is hungry for information. The spoken word nourishes the hungry soul. The audience wants a message that satisfies and sustains them. When you recite a speech the words are soon forgotten. When you deliver a message to people's hearts and minds, the audience will remember what you said for a long time, and sometimes it is a life-changing experience for someone. When you present a long list of thoughts and ideas that do not connect with people, it is like serving them a sandwich on stale bread with wilted lettuce. It's a problem. Great speakers use their voices effectively to deliver touching messages that hit home.

Your voice is your delivery instrument and can be used to create a desired effect. You cannot change the voice you were born with, but you can control how you use your voice. *Pace, phrasing, pauses,* and *pitch* are all under your control. When people are nervous, it is normal to speak too fast unintentionally. The nervousness makes the vocal cords get tighter, causing the voice to naturally rise in pitch. This is why remaining as calm as possible can enhance the overall delivery of your speech. If you get too nervous, you will not be speaking in your natural voice. Take a deep breath and find your natural voice, which sounds much better than your nervous voice. Rehearsing will help the nervousness. Practice in front of a large mirror and record your voice in order to hear what you sound like to an audience. This type of practice will also help improve your performance. Now, I know what you are thinking: I will look foolish practicing in front of a mirror. Consider the alternative—looking foolish and drowning in front of an audience of five hundred people. Practice in front of a large mirror. One day, you will thank me.

Everyone also has a natural pace, or tempo. When speaking at your natural pace, it is easier to eliminate annoying "uhs" in your speech and you can maintain greater continuity of thought. If you are not using notes, this helps your brain stay ahead of your mouth, which minimizes the "uhs," and if you are reading your speech, it helps you to create interesting phrasing in your delivery and allows you to emphasize key points appropriately. When you find your natural voice and natural pace, then your phrases and pauses will come naturally. However, variations in pace and pitch are highly recommended to prevent hypnotic monotony, which only puts people to sleep. And you will know when the audience is asleep. Even if there is no audible snore, they will all be staring straight ahead into space, their subconscious minds hoping that you will finish soon. This is not the effect you want as a speaker. So, practice!

Natural pitch, natural pace, natural phrasing, and natural pauses preceded by proper preparation will produce a great speech delivery. Now all you have to do is *project* your voice so people can hear you clearly. When people cannot hear you clearly, their minds wander and you lose their attention, which breaks the continuity of your message. Don't ask the audience if they can hear you. It's an unnecessary distraction, which takes away from your delivery. You should be able to hear your voice fill the room.

Even if you perfect all the P's—preparation, pitch, pace, phrasing, pauses, and projection—things can go wrong, but you can still give a great speech if you remain relaxed and focused.

The delivery of your speech is just as important as the substance (message) of your speech. The better you connect and captivate the audience and the better the delivery, the longer your substance will be remembered and the greater the impact you will have on people in the audience. As stated earlier, people absorb only fifty percent of what the speaker says, and two days later they remember only fifty percent of the fifty percent. On the other hand, if only one person in the audience remembers only one thing you said that helped them or changed their life, then your goal has been accomplished.

PRACTICE MAKES PERFECT

Whether I am at home in Omaha or traveling on business, I look forward to the first opportunity to hit the golf course. Golf is a great game. When I began golf as a hobby, I was not good at all. It took hours of practice to improve my game to a satisfactory level. I continue to practice in order to improve as much as I can. The same is true for building leadership skills and speaking skills. The more you make a focused effort, the more impressive you will be to your colleagues and before an audience. When you are ready to practice your speech, I suggest the following tips.

1. Practice your speech several times but do not try to memorize it. Memorization is pointless because you cannot predict what will happen once you are at the podium. If you practice several times, you will be familiar with the material and you will have the confidence to deliver your speech despite any unforeseen events.

2. Use a tape recorder to listen to your delivery. Are you speaking too quickly or too slowly? Is there a logical sequence to your ideas? Does it sound interesting to you?

3. If you plan to use slides, practice with the actual slides. Make sure that the slides are in the correct order.

4. Time your speech. You want to be sure that your twenty-minute address is not forty minutes. If it is forty minutes, revise it to fit the parameters of the meeting.

5. When possible, always get a video of your speech. Keep notes of your own critiques. This will help you with future speeches.

As the wise sage Socrates said, know yourself. Do what makes you comfortable in front of an audience. If you do prefer to read your speech word for word, then make sure you write it yourself. This will allow you to sound like it's your speech and to keep your eyes from becoming "glued to the paper."

As I have said before, one of the most effective ways to deliver a speech is to talk from an outline. This method allows you to be more conversational and extemporaneous. The outline can be written on index cards or displayed on slides. This obviously takes much practice to perfect, but it is the most effective technique for becoming a better speaker.

YOUR NATURAL STYLE IS A GOOD PLACE TO START

Inexperienced speakers are prone to making grave errors in front of an audience. Often, they try to overrelate to people. If you do this, you commit a sensitivity error or sound insincere. For example, a notable public figure was speaking to a convention of the United Negro College Fund. The audience was predominantly African American. In an attempt to connect with the audience, he tried to use the UNCF slogan, "A mind is a terrible thing to waste," in his speech. Instead of saying it correctly, he said, "It's a terrible thing to lose your mind." Oops! Obviously, the audience was not impressed.

It is easier to speak to an audience who does the same thing for a living as you do because every profession has a sublanguage that people in the profession understand. Mathematicians, as I described them earlier, talk in coefficients, equations, ballistics, pitch, and yaw. In the restaurant industry, we talk of sales, food costs, labor costs, quality, service, and cleanliness. Financial types talk in accounts, assets, liabilities, general ledgers, equities, and net worth. Computer types talk in bits, bytes, gigabytes, and operating hardware and software systems.

Different professions not only have different sublanguages, they also attract different personality types. This is why different audiences respond differently to humor, technical content, or even style of presentation. For example, I gave a keynote address to a group of mass retailers, which included department stores, discount stores, and general merchandise stores. This engagement had been booked through a speakers' bureau and they had provided me with information about the member companies. From the material I was provided, I thought I would be speaking to marketing and sales types, who are usually very responsive audiences because they must deal with the general public and customers on a daily basis. People attracted to the sales and marketing profession are usually more expressive and extroverted, so generally they laugh and respond spontaneously.

Unfortunately, I was not able to arrive the evening before the keynote to mingle with the attendees. After my speech, I discovered that the audience was not composed of sales and marketing types, but computer types—the people who ran the computer operations for the member retail companies. I worked as a computer type the first fifteen years of my professional career, so I feel qualified to describe them (most, not all) as introverts who view the world differently from many people.

Throughout my speech on leadership, I could feel their collective strained response to many of my stories and anecdotes. I use a self-grading system from one to ten to rate my speeches, with ten being the best. Afterward, I thought I had delivered a ten, and I'm extremely hard on myself, but the audience response was a seven in my judgment. Later that day I received feedback from the attendees that they had evaluated me as a ten. I was surprised.

Computer types may not respond higher than a seven even though they might think the speech is a ten. I simply did not know the audience, or I would not have been as concerned during my speech about the level of response. Secondly, had I known the audience correctly, I could have used different stories and anecdotes to drive home my message and key points better, which would have related to them more precisely.

I got a similar response from an audience of accounting types even though I was fully aware of the composition of the audience. I actually announced during my speech a couple of times that a particular comment was a joke, after which, they chuckled. Computer types and accounting types don't laugh; a chuckle is as good as it gets. They're just very analytical and serious by nature, which makes them good at what they do. But as the speaker, you need to know this ahead of time; otherwise, you might offend the audience or miss the audience completely.

My final piece of advice for new or experienced speakers is to ask the event coordinator or the speakers' bureau to send you a summary of the valuation forms and all the individual comments. After reading the comments, make a list of points for improvement. Incorporate one or two of these points in your next speech. Keep in mind that you will not be able to improve all areas at once. As you master each point through practice, go on to the next one. The more you practice and improve, the sharper you will be on the job and as the leader of your work team or organization.

LEADERS ARE ALWAYS PREPARED TO SPEAK

On a recent flight from Chicago to Atlanta with my son Vincent, who had heard me give a freenote address a few days earlier, he commented that he noticed that I must have a list of stories I choose from to include in my speeches. He mentioned this because he has heard me speak on several other occasions on the same topic, leadership. But some of the stories and anecdotes were different and they were used in different parts of the speech. I told him he was exactly right, because I try to customize the actual delivery to the audience as much as possible without changing the message.

Good speakers not only do the necessary pre-preparation for a speech, they are also prepared to "go with the flow" during their speech. Be prepared to modify the length of your speech by no more than ten minutes due to unexpected program changes or someone preceding you who did not read this book. "Modify" in this sense means to shorten your speech, because I have never been asked to speak longer. I use ten minutes as a rule of thumb, because to cut more than that out of a speech that was intended to be thirty minutes or more could drastically alter the outcome. When I experienced the speech from hell, I was able to refocus and pull it off because I had done that speech hundreds of times.

Sometimes during a speech, a story or anecdote will occur to me that was not planned but would effectively illustrate the point at hand. This is certainly risky (E factor), but it has the most impact when you feel comfortable doing so. Audiences with which you are very familiar are a good place to practice this technique. It is also especially useful if you are reading a prepared text, because it can break the inherent tendency to become monotonous.

Proper delivery and communication should not be limited only to formal speaking events, because getting the message across is critical even in the smallest group situation. As a leader and speaking as a leader, you are never offstage or off the record, which is why leaders are always honing their speaking skills.

THE UNSPOKEN WORD

Nonverbal communication complements the spoken word and can help connect with the audience or keep them totally disconnected. A book that I recommend on this subject is *Body Language* by Julius Fast. This book was deeply informative and helpful to me as I developed my speaking skills. Awareness of the nonverbal part of speaking will help you avoid talking to the back wall of the room, clutching the podium with a death grip, eyes glued to the paper, golf-ball-size beads of sweat popping off your forehead, a voice pitch capable of breaking crystal, or wearing an outfit that only a mother could love, to name just a few. In fact, an important aspect of the speech delivery is nonverbal. Your attire, posture, facial expressions, gestures, and even your pauses make no sound at all. But their impact on your speech delivery can be as loud as a siren. Generally speaking, you want to look "professional," which does not tell you much, since different people interpret the phrase differently. Find out which styles and colors look best on you. For example, I never wear brown because to me, I look and feel like I am just blending in with a dead tree—how boring. My best suit colors are blue and black with properly coordinated shirts and ties. Most important, everything must fit properly to complement your neatly groomed hair and shined shoes, because someone is going to notice your hair and your shoes.

Posture should simply be erect but not at military attention. Gestures and facial expressions should be as natural as possible. If you have no natural gesture, then at least move your arms and hands occasionally so the audience will know that you are not dead. Try to look directly at someone in the audience if it does not throw you off.

Using the unspoken word effectively is no different from using the spoken word effectively; it just takes practice and more practice.

IT'S SHOW TIME! (*SPEECH OCCASIONS*)

You have crafted a great *message* (shape, shake, and bake), planned a great date with your *audience,* and eliminated all known technical distractions—it is now "show time!" Each type of speaking occasion is slightly different and offers a new opportunity to make a great *delivery.*

Ten types of speaking occasions that require different considerations in order to achieve maximum effectiveness in delivery are:

1. Keynote address
2. Business presentation
3. Banquet or luncheon
4. Staff meeting
5. Committee report

6. Press interview
7. Master of ceremony
8. Impromptu remarks
9. Outdoor event
10. All other speaking occasions

The *keynote address* is the most important of speeches because it could be your last one if you blow it. Keynotes should have a memorable title, contain three key points or less, and be forty-five minutes or less in length. Expectations are high since it is a keynote, so winging it is not recommended. If you haven't delivered the speech before, then find someone to listen to you practice and to provide you with feedback. The use of visual support materials is a function of content and individual style, especially if the presentation is technical, but visual aids need to be neat, clear, and large enough to see plainly from all parts of the room.

A keynote address can be delivered effectively in a minimum of twenty minutes. An average speech (rating of five to six) can survive thirty minutes because that's when people start checking how long you have talked, but if you go forty minutes, the speech should be in the seven to eight rating category. A forty- to fifty-minute keynote speech should be a nine to ten rating, or you have reached the point of diminishing memorability. In the unusual instances when you are asked to give a keynote longer than an hour, then bring dancing bears or other animals that do tricks. The other options are to talk no more than an hour or have a planned question and answer time. If you do a Q&A session, then hope that the last question is a good one so you can end on "message" and on a positive note, or have a planned closing comment, quote, or story.

The *business presentation* begins with an objective, such as to persuade, communicate, close the sale, or establish the groundwork for future decisions. Unlike the keynote address, the business presentation allows and encourages interactions during the presentation. If presenting to superiors in the organization, you can assume there will be interruptions, so you really have to keep the presentation moving and on track. If the allotted time is a half hour or less, then visuals are optional. If the allotted time is more than a half hour, then visual aids are highly recommended. In both cases, a "leave-behind" document is recommended. Always present in less than the allotted time *unless* the audience extends the time with questions.

Banquet and luncheon speeches are very similar but an audience tends to be less attentive at an evening banquet. Most people will have had a full day and a cocktail or two, and the last thing they want to hear is a long, boring speech. Therefore, banquet and luncheon speeches should be succinct and as entertaining as you feel comfortable making them. If you are the main speaker, it is not advisable to speak while food is being served or while people are eating their entrée. Most groups will accommodate such a request, as well as a request that no further service to the tables be made during your speech. Try to connect or relate to something else said or done on the program to show you are paying attention and never criticize the food or accommodations. Spontaneous humor works best if you are good at it, otherwise, just be pleasant and make sure the audience leaves with a few nuggets of information.

At breakfast, luncheon, or dinner speeches, the audience appreciates light learning and heavy entertaining. If you develop a repertoire of key messages, you can customize the message for the occasion. If you are not good at entertaining, just keep it informative and short. For noneating speaking occasions, audiences expect a little heavier learning (informative), but they'd still like the entertainment to be high. Your goal is more than just keeping them awake. Your goal is to inspire them to think about your message in relation to their work environment and personal lives.

In a typical *staff meeting,* I strongly recommend that you show up with a written list of points you want to discuss. This keeps the meeting focused. Obviously, one point that should always be included is open discussion, since staff meetings should encourage dialogue and not just monologue. Maintain eye contact because it conveys confidence and sincerity. Sitting at a conference table with small groups is more conversational, but it may be necessary to stand for larger groups. Above all, don't waste your people's time, because they have work to do.

An effective *committee report* should give highlights, lowlights, action items, and any follow-up intended, then sit down. If the group had wanted the entire committee discussion rehashed, then they would not have established a committee, and you would not be giving the committee report.

Although a *press interview* is not a speech per se, there are three tips to keep in mind. First, if you know the topic ahead of time, plan the key points you want to make during the interview and be able to state those points in a variety of ways. If you will be doing frequent interviews with the press, then a media training course would be advisable in order to learn effective communication techniques. Second, there is no such thing as off the record. If you say it, then assume it might be used at some point. Third, expect the unexpected and be prepared to remain calm and professional.

Shortly after the release of my book *Leadership Is Common Sense*, I was interviewed on a New York television station. The reporter had read the book and questioned me about the leadership principles. He had read the section where I described my 1994 town hall meeting encounter with President Clinton. Suddenly, the reporter said, "You don't like President Clinton very much, do you?" With a brief pause, I responded that liking him or not was not the issue relative to his leadership of this country. The reporter then asked, "Is President Clinton a great leader?" I responded, "He's a great politician."

In both instances, I did not answer the questions directly, because the reporter was trying to draw me into a personal attack on the president with the first question and was looking for me to indict the president's leadership with the second question. If I had answered those questions directly, it would have been too easy for those sound bites to show up somewhere else totally out of context. Expect the unexpected and learn when to answer indirectly.

When you are the *emcee,* your purpose is to complement the program not compliment yourself. You are responsible for the opening, closing, and continuity of the program. This is best achieved by getting to know the program content and participants ahead of time, which also helps if some unexpected changes should occur during the program. Anybody can just read what's on the printed program, so try to add something by way of some relevant comments, quotes, or stories, but by all means, don't talk too much.

If you are asked to give *impromptu remarks,* do not experiment.

Go with your instincts and what is already in your repertoire. If it is an *outdoor event,* don't try to compete with Mother Nature. Be brief and witty and sit down. For *all other speaking occasions,* such as graduation speeches, acceptance speeches, or rejection speeches, brevity and simplicity are key.

You will notice that I did not include panel discussions in my list of primary speaking occasions. I personally do not like to do panels, because while they are intended to present different points of view, they usually just show off different personalities, and you are usually constrained to a few sound bites. But if you choose to do them, treat them like a press interview. The few panels I have done have worked best when panelists have been able to meet and compare intended comments in advance. Otherwise, everyone is just winging it without coordination.

When it's "show time," seize the moment. Seize the moment to demonstrate how well you have prepared your message. Seize the moment to illustrate how well you have gotten to know the audience. Seize the moment to show how much you are in command of the technical parameters and how much practice has gone into your delivery. Seize the moment to connect and captivate the audience for a mutually exhilarating experience, and seize the moment to possibly change someone's life.

In short, seize the moment to "speak as a leader."

CHAPTER 5

An Analysis of Three Great Speeches:

Gettysburg Address, Abraham Lincoln, 1863

Independence Day Address, Frederick Douglass, 1852

The Berlin Crisis, John F. Kennedy, 1961

THERE HAVE BEEN MANY GREAT speeches that have inspired people, caused people to take action, or caused people not to take certain undesirable action, such as war. One thing that all great speeches have in common is the intended message is crystal clear and most often very memorable.

Dr. Martin Luther King's speech "I Have a Dream" still resonates today because his message transcended politics, race, and ethnic origin. Many people may not be able to quote long passages from his speech, but the depth of his message is undeniable. Great speeches sometimes produce great memorable quotes, which reinforce the message over time.

Another common characteristic of great speeches is that they follow the general pattern discussed in this book, which I will illustrate with an analysis of three great speeches. These speeches are three of my all-time favorites. Obviously, this is not with respect to the actual delivery, since I was not even born in 1852 or 1863, but, rather, these analyses focus on the very powerful structural content and message of each speech. I must admit that I applied the principles of this book to these speeches after I put my approach to speaking down on paper and was pleasantly surprised at how consistently these great speeches by these three great leaders were so similarly structured.

Gettysburg Address
1863

Lincoln's Gettysburg Address demonstrates that a great speech does not have to be long.

OPENING:

> Four score and seven years ago, our fathers brought forth upon this continent a new nation: conceived in liberty, and dedicated to the proposition that all men are created equal.

INFORM:

> Now we are engaged in a great civil war . . . testing whether that nation, or any nation so conceived and so dedicated . . . can long endure. We are met on a great battlefield of that war.
>
> We have come to dedicate a portion of that field as a final resting place for those who here gave their lives that this nation might live. It is altogether fitting and proper that we should do this.

ENGAGE:

> But, in a larger sense, we cannot dedicate . . . we cannot consecrate . . . we cannot hallow this ground. The brave men, living and dead, who struggled here have consecrated it, far above our poor power to add or detract. The world will little note, nor long remember, what we say here, but it can never forget what they did here.

INSPIRE:

> It is for us the living, rather, to be dedicated here to the unfinished work which they who fought here have thus far so nobly advanced. It is, rather, for us to be here dedicated to the great task remaining before us . . . that from these honored dead we take increased devotion to that cause for which they gave the last full measure of devotion. . . .

CLOSING:

> . . . that we here highly resolve that these dead shall not have died in vain . . . that this nation, under God, shall have a new birth of freedom . . . and that government of the people . . . by the people . . . for the people . . . shall not perish from this earth.

The apparent structure of Lincoln's address is almost too good to be true. It correlates perfectly and succinctly with the most compelling components of opening, inform, engage, inspire, and closing. Most people are familiar with Lincoln's famous opening of "Four score and seven years ago" and his timeless close of "government of the people, by the people, for the people." But the most powerful component of Lincoln's address is how he *engaged* the audience by symbolically contradicting the very reason they were supposed to be assembled, namely, the occasion was to dedicate the field where many had died for the cause of freedom, but then he goes on to say that "in a larger sense, we cannot dedicate." This most certainly stirs the interest and curiosity of the audience as to what he means, which he so eloquently articulates: "the brave men, living and dead" have already consecrated this field "far above our poor power to add or detract." Now, that's engaging!

One of Lincoln's greatest challenges as a leader was to constantly *inspire* the nation not to surrender its principles of freedom and unity despite the horrors of war. Lincoln successfully met that challenge.

INDEPENDENCE DAY ADDRESS
1852

The Independence Day Address by Frederick Douglass on July 4, 1852, is a riveting example of the power of the spoken *and* written word. The mere setting of an escaped slave speaking to a white audience so forthrightly, eleven years before the Emancipation Proclamation, is by itself compelling and captivating.

Another interesting thing about Douglass's speech is that he did not try to sugar coat the absolute contradiction of his presence there that day. Namely, he states directly to the audience that "this fourth of July is yours, not mine. You may rejoice, I must mourn."

Unlike most speeches, Douglass's does not *inspire* the audience with the disparity between us. In fact, he does just the opposite of inspiring, which I call *despiring,* all the way through to the end of the speech. The forum and components of the speech are, however, similar to that described in this book with lots of "condiments" (oratorical beauty) around his key points.

He *engages* the audience many times with such passages as:

> "Fellow citizens, above your national, tumultuous joy, I hear the mournful wail of millions!"
>
> "I shall see this day and its popular characteristics from the slave's point of view."
>
> "Fellow citizens, pardon me, allow me to ask, why am I called upon to speak here today? What have I, or those I represent, to do with your national independence?"

After three opening paragraphs to set his tone for his speech, he then has two paragraphs that draw (engage) his audience into his upcoming line of reasoning. The next five paragraphs are some of the most captivating, riveting, and gripping passages ever written. I describe some of his passages as pounding a stake right into the heart of slavery in America:

"America is false to the past, false to the present and solemnly binds itself to be false to the future."

"Slavery—the great sin and shame of America."

"Must I undertake to prove that the slave is a man?"

"The manhood of the slave is conceded. It is admitted in the fact that the Southern statute books are covered with enactments, forbidding under severe fines and penalties, the teaching of the slave to read or write. When you can point to any such laws in reference to the beasts of the field, then I may consent to argue the manhood of the slave."

Powerful! In other words, until there are also laws to deny animals to read and write and other rights, Douglass is not even willing to debate the manhood of the slave. In fact, the manhood of the slave has already been conceded by the mere fact that so many laws existed at the time denying the citizenship of the slave.

The closing two paragraphs do not let the audience off the hook with a typical uplifting close. They are *despiring* and penetrating:

"There is not a nation on the earth guilty of practices more shocking and bloody than are the people of the United States at this very hour."

". . . for revolting barbarity and shameless hypocrisy, America reigns without a rival."

For me, the only thing that could surpass the powerful impact of reading Douglass's speech would have been to hear him deliver it on that day. But then, I would have been born a slave and not a free man.

OPENING:

Fellow citizens, pardon me, allow me to ask, Why am I called upon to speak here today? What have I, or those I represent, to do with your national independence? Are the great principles of political freedom and of natural justice, embodied in that Declaration of Independence, extended to us? And am I, therefore, called upon to bring our humble offering to the national altar and to confess the benefits and express devout gratitude for the blessings resulting from your independence to us?

Would to God, both for your sakes and ours, that an affirmative answer could be truthfully returned to these questions! Then would my task be light and my burden easy and delightful. For who is there so cold that a nation's sympathy could not warm him? Who so obdurate and dead to the claims of gratitude that would not thankfully acknowledge such priceless benefits? Who so stolid and selfish that would not give his voice to swell the hallelujahs of a nation's jubilee, when the chains of servitude had been torn from his limbs? I am not that man. In a case like that the dumb might eloquently speak and the "lame man leap as a hart."

INFORM:

But such is not the state of the case. I say it with a sad sense of the disparity between us. I am not included within the pale of this glorious anniversary! Your high independence only reveals the immeasurable distance between us. The blessings in which you, this day, rejoice are not enjoyed in common. The rich inheritance of justice, liberty, prosperity, and independence bequeathed by your fathers is shared by you, not by me. The sunlight that brought light and healing to you has brought stripes and death to me. This Fourth of July is yours, not mine. You may rejoice, I must mourn. To drag a man in fetters into the grand illuminated temple of liberty, and call upon him to join you in joyous anthems, were inhuman mockery, sacrilegious irony. Do you mean, citizens, to mock me by asking me to speak today? If so, there is a parallel to your conduct. And let me warn you that it is dangerous to copy the example of a nation whose crimes, towering up to the heaven, were thrown down by the breath of the Almighty, burying that nation in irrevocable ruin! I can today take up the plaintive lament of a peeled and woe-smitten people! . . .

ENGAGE:

Fellow citizens, above your national, tumultuous joy, I hear the mournful wail of millions!—whose chains, heavy and grievous yesterday, are, today, rendered more intolerable by the jubilee shouts that reach them. If I do forget, if I do not faithfully remember those bleeding children of sorrow this day, "may my right hand forget her cunning, and may my evil tongue cleave to the roof of my mouth"! To forget them, to pass lightly over their wrongs, and to chime in with the popular theme would be treason most scandalous and shocking, and would make me a reproach before God and the world.

My subject, then, fellow citizens, is American slavery. I shall see this day and its popular characteristics from the slave's point of view. Standing there identified with the American bondman, making his wrongs mine. I do not hesitate to declare with all my soul that the character and conduct of this nation never looked blacker to me than on this Fourth of July! Whether we turn to the declarations of the past or the professions of the present, the conduct of the nation seems equally hideous and revolting.

CAPTIVATING:

America is false to the past, false to the present, and solemnly binds herself to be false to the future. Standing with God and the crushed and bleeding slave on this occasion, I will, in the name of humanity which is outraged, in the name of liberty which is fettered, in the name of the Constitution and the Bible which are disregarded and trampled upon, dare to call in question and to denounce, with all the emphasis I can command, everything that serves to perpetuate slavery—the great sin and shame of America! . . .

But I fancy I hear someone of my audience say, "It is just in this circumstance that you and your brother abolitionists fail to make a favorable impression on the public mind. Would you argue more and enounce less, would you persuade more and rebuke less, your cause would be much more likely to succeed."

But, I submit, where all is plain, there is nothing to be argued. What point in the antislavery creed would you have me argue? On what branch of the subject do the people of this country need light? Must I undertake to prove that the slave is a man? That point is conceded already. Nobody doubts it. The slaveholders themselves acknowledge it in the enactment of laws for their government. They acknowledge it when they punish disobedience on the part of the slave. There are seventy-two crimes in the state of Virginia which, if committed by a black man (no matter how ignorant he be), subject him to the punishment of death; while only two of the same crimes will subject a white man to the like punishment. What is this but the acknowledgment that a slave is a moral, intellectual, and responsible being? The manhood of the slave is conceded. It is admitted in the fact that the Southern statute books are covered with enactments forbidding, under severe fines and penalties, the teaching of the slave to read or to write. When you can point to any such laws in reference to the beasts of the field, then I may consent to argue the manhood of the slave. When the dogs in your streets, when the fowls of the air, when the cattle on your hills, when the fish of the sea and the reptiles that crawl shall be unable to distinguish the slave from a brute, then will I argue with you that the slave is a man!

For the present, it is enough to affirm the equal manhood of the Negro race. Is it not astonishing that, while we are plowing, planting, and reaping, using all kinds of mechanical tools, erecting houses, constructing bridges, building ships, working in metals of brass, iron, copper, silver, and gold; that, while we are reading, writing, and ciphering, acting as clerks, merchants, and secretaries, having among us lawyers, doctors, ministers, poets, authors, editors, orators, and teachers; that, while we are engaged in all manner of enterprises common to other men, digging gold in California, capturing the whale in the Pacific, feeding sheep and cattle on the hillside, living, moving, acting, thinking, planning, living in families as husbands, wives, and children, and above all, confessing and worshiping the Christian's God, and looking hopefully for life and immortality beyond the grave, we are called upon to prove that we are men!

What, am I to argue that it is wrong to make men brutes, to rob them of their liberty, to work them without wages, to keep them ignorant of their relations to their fellow men. To beat them with sticks, to flay their flesh with the lash, to lead their limbs with irons, to hunt them with dogs, to sell them at auction, to sunder their families, to knock our their teeth, to burn their flesh, to starve them into obedience and submission to their masters? Must I argue that a system thus marked with blood, and stained with pollution, is wrong? No! I will not. I have better employment for my time and strength than such arguments would imply.

What, then, remains to be argued? Is it that slavery is not divine; that God did not establish it; that our doctors of divinity are mistaken? There is blasphemy in the thought. That which is inhuman cannot be divine! Who can reason on such a proposition? They that can may; I cannot. The time for such argument is past . . .

DESPIRING:

What, to the American slave, is your Fourth of July? I answer: a day that reveals to him, more than all other days in the year, the gross injustice and cruelty to which he is the constant victim. To him, your celebration is a sham; your boasted liberty, an unholy license; your national greatness, swelling vanity; your sounds of rejoicing are empty and heartless; your denunciation of tyrants, brass-fronted impudence; your shouts of liberty and quality, hollow mockery; your prayers and hymns, your sermons and thanksgivings, with all your religious parade and solemnity, are, to him, mere bombast, fraud, deception, impiety, and hypocrisy—a thin veil to cover up crimes which would disgrace a nation of savages. There is not a nation of savages. There is not a nation on the earth guilty of practices more shocking and bloody than are the people of the United States at this very house.

DESPIRING CLOSING:

Go where you may, search where you will, roam through all the monarchies and despotism of the Old World, travel through

South America, search out every abuse, and when you have found the last, lay your facts by the side of the everyday practices of this nation, and you will say with me that, for revolting barbarity and shameless hypocrisy, America reigns without a rival.

THE BERLIN CRISIS
1961

The Berlin Crisis speech by John F. Kennedy is noticeably and appropriately longer than the other two speeches analyzed in this section. It is difficult to avert what could have ignited a third world war with a few sound bites.

Structurally, Kennedy's speech does all the right things and is loaded with much more information and is much more engaging than a typical speech. I would venture to say that it was entirely necessary so as to make sure that the Russians, and particularly Khrushchev, knew that the United States was deadly serious. This depth of *inform* and *engage* was also necessary to make sure the American people understood the severity of the crisis and what we were prepared to do if necessary. Just notice the six *inform* paragraphs following the *opening* paragraph, and then eight engaging paragraphs that keep you on the edge of your seat. Kennedy then returns to another short *inform* paragraph that says he's not bluffing and that peace or war is in Khrushchev's hands if he tries to confiscate West Berlin.

Kennedy exemplified all the critical characteristics of leadership and all the critical things a leader must do in this Berlin crisis incident. He was self-motivated to take the lead in countering the Russians' threat to just declare West Berlin a part of the communist world despite the fact that the allied powers had won the right in World War II for West Germany to be a democracy. He took a risk in telling Khrushchev exactly what we were prepared to do even before getting the formal support of Congress. His respect as president by the American people and Congress allowed him to take that risk and, ultimately, get their full support.

Kennedy's *focus* was clear, namely, "we seek peace but we will not surrender the right of two million people to determine their own future and choose their own way of life." The barrier he *removed* was the barrier of doubt that the United States would do whatever necessary to preserve democracy and freedom. He was working on the right problem, the threat of war, and obtained the right result in the end—peace.

The American people were *inspired* because they had the confidence that he was doing the right thing.

OPENING:

> Seven weeks ago tonight I returned from Europe to report on my meeting with Premier Khrushchev and the others. His grim warnings about the future of the world, his aide-mémoire on Berlin, his subsequent speeches and threats which he and his agents have launched, and the increase in the Soviet military budget that he has announced have all prompted a series of decisions by the administration and a series of consultations with the members of the NATO organization. In Berlin, as you recall, he intends to bring to an end, through a stroke of the pen, first our legal rights to be in West Berlin and secondly our ability to make good on our commitment to the two million free people of that city. That we cannot permit . . .

INFORM:

> West Berlin is one hundred ten miles within the area which the Soviets now dominate—which is immediately controlled by the so-called East German regime . . . We are there as a result of our victory over Nazi Germany—and our basic rights to be there deriving from that victory include both our presence in West Berlin and the enjoyment of access across East Germany. These rights have been repeatedly confirmed and recognized in special agreements with the Soviet Union. Berlin is not a part of East Germany but a separate territory under the control of allied powers. Thus our rights there are clear and deep-rooted. But in addition to those rights is our commitment

to sustain—and defend, if need be—the opportunity for more than two million people to determine their own future and choose their own way of life.

Thus, our presence in West Berlin, and our access thereto, cannot be ended by any act of the Soviet government. The NATO shield was long ago extended to cover West Berlin—and we have given our word that an attack in that city will be regarded as an attack upon us all.

For West Berlin—lying exposed one hundred ten miles inside East Germany, surrounded by Soviet troops and close to Soviet supply lines—has many roles. It is more than a showcase of liberty, a symbol, an island of freedom in a Communist sea. It is even more than a link with the Free World, a beacon of hope behind the Iron Curtain, an escape hatch for refugees.

West Berlin is all of that. But above all it has now become—as never before—the great testing place of Western courage and will, a focal point where our solemn commitments stretching back over the years since 1945 and Soviet ambitions now meet in basic confrontation.

It would be a mistake for others to look upon Berlin, because of its location, as a tempting target. The United States is there; the United Kingdom and France are there; the pledge of NATO is there—and the people of Berlin are there. It is as secure, in that sense, as the rest of us—for we cannot separate its safety from our own.

We do not want to fight, but we have fought before. And others in earlier times have made the same dangerous mistake of assuming that the West was too selfish and too soft and too divided to resist invasions of freedom in other lands. Those who threaten to unleash the forces of war on a dispute over West Berlin should recall the words of the ancient philosopher: "A man who causes fear cannot be free from fear."

ENGAGE:

So long as the Communists insist that they are preparing to end by themselves unilaterally our rights in West Berlin and our commitments to its people, we must be prepared to defend those rights and those commitments. We will at all times be ready to talk, if talk will help. But we must also be ready to resist with force, if force is used upon us. Either alone would fail. Together, they can serve the cause of freedom and peace . . .

Thus, in the days and months ahead, I shall not hesitate to ask the Congress for additional measures or exercise any of the executive powers that I possess to meet this threat to peace. Everything essential to the security of freedom must be done; and if that should require more men, or more taxes, or more controls, or other new powers, I shall not hesitate to ask them. The measures proposed today will be constantly studied and altered as necessary. But while we will not let panic shape our policy, neither will we permit timidity to direct our program.

Accordingly, I am now taking the following steps:

1. I am tomorrow requesting the Congress for the current fiscal year an additional $3.247 billion of appropriations for the armed forces.

2. To fill out our present army divisions, and to make more men available for prompt deployment, I am requesting an increase in the army's total authorized strength from 875,000 to approximately one million men.

3. I am requesting an increase of 29,000 and 63,000 men respectively in the active duty strength of the navy and the air force.

4. To fulfill these manpower needs, I am ordering that our draft calls be doubled and tripled in the coming months; I am asking the Congress for authority to order to active duty certain ready reserve units and individual reservists, and to extend tours of duty; and, under that authority, I am planning to order to active duty a number of air transport squadrons and Air National Guard tactical air squadrons, to give us the air-lift capacity and protection that we need. Other reserve forces will be called up when needed.

5. Many ships and planes once headed for retirement are to be retained or reactivated, increasing our air power tactically and our sea-lift, air-lift, and antisubmarine warfare capability. In addition, our strategic air power will be increased by delaying the deactivation of B-47 bombers.

6. Finally, some $1.8 billion—about half of the total sum—

is needed for the procurement of non-nuclear weapons, ammunition, and equipment . . .

To recognize the possibilities of nuclear war in the missile age, without our citizens knowing what they should do and where they should go if bombs begin to fall, would be a failure of responsibility. In May, I pledged a new start on civil defense. Last week, I assigned, on the recommendation of the civil defense director, basic responsibility for this program to the secretary of defense, to make certain it is administered and coordinated with our continental defense efforts at the highest civilian level. Tomorrow, I am requesting of the Congress new funds for the following immediate objectives: to identify and mark space in existing structures—public and private—that could be used for fallout shelters in case of attack; to stock those shelters with food, water, first-aid kits, and other minimum essentials for survival; to increase their capacity; to improve our air-raid warning and fallout detection systems, including a new household warning system which is now under development; and to take other measures that will be effective at an early date to save millions of lives if needed.

In the event of an attack, the lives of those families which are not hit in a nuclear blast and fire can still be saved—if they can be warned to take shelter and if that shelter is available. We owe that kind of insurance to our families—and to our country. In contrast to our friends in Europe, the need for this kind of protection is new to our shores. But the time to start is now. In the coming months, I hope to let every citizen know what steps he can take without delay to protect his family in case of attack. I know that you will want to do no less . . .

But I must emphasize again that the choice is not merely between resistance and retreat, between atomic holocaust and surrender. Our peacetime military posture is traditionally defensive; but our diplomatic posture need not be. Our response to the Berlin crisis will not be merely military or negative. I will be more than merely standing firm. For we do not intend to leave it to others to choose and monopolize the forum and the framework of discussion. We do not intend to abandon our duty to mankind to seek a peaceful solution . . .

We recognize the Soviet Union's historical concerns about their security in Central and Eastern Europe, after a series of ravaging invasions—and we believe arrangements can be worked out which will help to meet those concerns and make it possible for both security and freedom to exist in this troubled area.

For it is not the freedom of West Berlin which is "abnormal" in Germany today, but the situation in that entire divided country. If anyone doubts the legality of our rights in Berlin, we are ready to have it submitted to international adjudication. If anyone doubts the extent to which our presence is desired by the people of West Berlin, compared to East German feelings about their regime, we are ready to have that question submitted to a free vote in Berlin and, if possible, among all the German people. And let us hear at that time from the two and one-half million refugees who have fled the Communist regime in East Germany—voting for Western-type freedom with their feet . . .

INFORM:

The solemn vow each of us gave to West Berlin in time of peace will not be broken in time of danger. If we do not meet our commitments to Berlin, where will we later stand? If we are not true to our word there, all that we have achieved in collective security, which relies on these words, will mean nothing. And if there is one path above all others to war, it is the path of weakness and disunity.

INSPIRE:

Today, the endangered frontier of freedom runs through divided Berlin. We want it to remain a frontier of peace. This is the hope of every citizen of the Atlantic Community; every citizen of Eastern Europe; and, I am confident, every citizen of the Soviet Union. For I cannot believe that the Russian people—who bravely suffered enormous losses in the Second World War—would now wish to see the peace upset once more in Germany. The Soviet government alone can convert Berlin's frontier of peace into a pretext for war.

CLOSING:

The steps I have indicated tonight are aimed at avoiding that war. To sum it all up: we seek peace—but we shall not surrender. That is the central meaning of this crisis—and the meaning of your government's policy.

With your help, and the help of other free men, this crisis can be surmounted. Freedom can prevail—and peace can endure.

CHAPTER 6

My Three Best Speeches . . . So Far

Get on the Wagon, Godfather's Pizza, Inc.

Big Potatoes, Godfather's Pizza, Inc.

Save the Frog, a Message on Restoring Free Enterprise

MY THREE BEST SPEECHES . . . so far . . . were each inspired by a critical event that occurred during my career. Each speech was written and delivered with the intended purpose of inspiring the listeners to believe they could influence an outcome and that they could take specific actions to that end.

"Get on the Wagon" was my first speech to the entire Godfather's Pizza company. I had already captivated their attention by the mere fact that I was the new president of the company, and the day-long meeting had been structured to be very informative and interactive. The event was the start of my leadership of the company in which I would "turn the company around." This speech delivered at the end of the meeting was my opportunity to show the attendees why they should believe in the new strategy and to inspire them to make it happen. By successfully conveying my own belief and self-motivation with a sincerely passionate delivery, the speech was a success.

GET ON THE WAGON, GODFATHER'S PIZZA, INC., MAY 29, 1986

Over the last two days we have brought you up to date on what has happened during the first sixty days of a new beginning. These sixty days have redefined our direction for the next sixty months. Therefore, a final challenge is in order.

As such, I want to challenge each of you to do three things which will change our individual and collective futures if you choose to accept this call for action.

First, I challenge each of you to dream again. The turbulence of the last three years has dampened your ability to envision goals and achievements beyond the problems of the day.

The feelings you experienced when business was declining—while your competitor's performance was increasing—stifled your ability to creatively attack problems and turn them into opportunities.

Lack of focus and clarity have poisoned your desire to aspire for possibilities beyond your grasp.

We believe focus has been established. As we evolve out of our entrepreneurial state into a more stable and structured existence, we believe that our business can once again thrive and that turbulence has now been replaced with order, direction, and positive intensity.

Therefore, I challenge you to dream again of possibilities beyond your grasp. I challenge you to dream of success, prosperity, and personal fulfillment once again. When you allow yourself to dream, you look at a mound of clay and see a masterpiece. You look at a glass of water half empty as a glass half filled. When you dream again, you are able to recognize that problems are merely dangerous opportunities that could unlock the doors to your success. When you dream again, you view today as the first day of the rest of your life. I challenge you to dream of Godfather's in 1990 as the number one pizza chain in the world. And if you truly do dream of being a part of that achievement, your creative energies will be unleashed and unstoppable. I challenge you to dream again about what Godfather's can become.

Secondly, I challenge each of you to commit yourself to the task before us, as others have already committed to your success.

Sixty days ago I came to Godfather's with a curiosity about what I would find. I had already accepted my newly bestowed responsibilities even before I stepped foot on Nebraska soil and before I met or knew anyone or anything about Godfather's. I also came sixty days ago with a one hundred-day plan as to how we would formulate a plan of action for the future. Sixty days ago, I came to Godfather's anxious to tackle a situation considered by some of our external constituencies to be irreversible. I came without a golden parachute because I never entertained the idea that the situation was irreversible. I came committed to prove the skeptics wrong because I have a personal, fundamental belief in the power of human determination. I came to Godfather's believing in you even before I met you. I challenge you to commit and believe in yourself and Godfather's Pizza as a system.

When I arrived at Godfather's Pizza on April 1, 1986, I found there were others who believed victory could be ours. I found people who were not only personally committed but who also possessed ideas, skills, capabilities, and the tenacity necessary to accomplish the job ahead of us. Members of our management team and your own elected Franchise Advisory Council made it possible for us to achieve the one hundred–day plan in twenty-five days. Within the last sixty days, about six months of work has been completed—six months' work in sixty days because they shared the belief and commitment that we can and will succeed.

In addition, there are those like myself who have joined our effort knowing only that we would be engaged in a competitive fight for our lives and not knowing the magnitude of our ammunition or the severity of the enemy.

One of the questions asked by some franchisees during my early days at Godfather's was "What is the commitment of Pillsbury?" Pillsbury's commitment is best summarized by what it could do but has not done. Namely, because of the relatively minimal financial investment in Godfather's, Pillsbury could eliminate Godfather's from its books as a tax write-off with a stroke of a bean-counter's pen and barely miss a step—if it so desired. But Pillsbury does not desire to do so. Obviously, Pillsbury's commitment is much greater than just dollars and cents.

I challenge you to commit yourself to the task before us as others have already committed to your success.

The third, and concluding challenge to every Godfather's corporate employee, to every operator, to every owner, to every restaurant manager, to every crew member, to every person connected in any way to the Godfather's system is "Let's go." Let's get on with rewriting the currently anticipated future of Godfather's in the annals of the restaurant industry.

There are generally three kinds of people in the world. People who make things happen, people who watch things happen, and people who say "What in the hell happened?"

People who make things happen—they dream. People who make things happen—they commit themselves. People who make things happen say "Let's go."

If we are to be successful, we must agree to listen to one another. We must agree to disagree with one another but agree to support and move with the majority as a system.

In the last two days we have described what we believed to be a start in the right direction. We do not know absolutely if it is one hundred percent right, nor do we claim to have all the answers. But fact, logic, experience, collective thinking, and our gut tell us that it is at least eighty percent right, which when added to one hundred percent teamwork will produce two hundred percent success . . . if we all say "Let's go." We must, and will, be on a different timetable.

As one anonymous author wrote: "Life is just a minute— only sixty seconds in it. Forced upon me—can't refuse it. Didn't seek it. Didn't choose it. But it's up to me to use it. I must suffer if I lose it—give an account if I abuse it. Just a tiny little minute but eternity is in it."

I realize that this timetable may be too fast for some, and I realize that the objectives may be too aggressive for many. And I realize that the war we are about to wage may be too bloody and risky for some. But to paraphrase the motto of the United States Marine Corps, we are looking for a few good people. We will be successful with a few good people who have the inner vision to dream. We will be successful with a few good people who have the tenacity to commit. We will be successful with a few good people with the desire to aspire to make things happen by accepting the challenge "Let's go."

Let's yank victory from the jaws of defeat!

People! People! People! Apart we are weak. Together we are strong.

In the unforgettable words of my grandfather, a Georgia farmer all his life who would hitch a team of mules to the wagon on Saturdays for the weekly trip into the local town: "Them that's going—get on the wagon ... them that ain't—get out of the way."

Them that's going—get on the wagon . . . them that ain't—get out of the way!

We had successfully achieved the "turnaround of Godfather's" much faster than most people ever expected, including the parent company, Pillsbury! But the turnaround was only in sales, profitability, and morale. The long-term capital investment needs of Godfather's had to be addressed in order to sustain the turnaround. Pillsbury decided not to make these investments in such things as store remodels, technology, and new restaurants to increase penetration in key markets. As a result, Pillsbury decided to sell Godfather's.

I was informed of Pillsbury's decision in January 1988, at which time, Ron Gartlan and I decided to make an effort to buy Godfather's with a leveraged buyout. With Pillsbury's help and a lot of stressful months, we completed the transaction in September 1988.

During these eight and a half months, the Godfather's organization was, understandably, distracted. In anticipation of closing the transaction sometime in August 1988, we scheduled another all-systems meeting for September to refocus the company after the long period of completing the buyout. Due to some issues with the lending institution that had to be resolved, we did not complete the closing on the buyout until September 16, 1988, the same day the all-systems meeting was planned to start.

Ron Gartlan, Gary Batenhorst, and I completed signing all the documents in New York at about 12:30 P.M., rushed to the airport to fly to Tampa, Florida, in hopes of making the opening reception of the 1988 Godfather's convention. We made it.

Obviously, everyone was eager to know if it was a done deal. When we entered the room, we moved forward to the front. I went to the microphone and said, "At approximately twelve-thirty this afternoon, we closed the leveraged buyout and we are now the new, heavily in debt owners of Godfather's Pizza, Inc." After a long and enthusiastic round of applause, I simply said, "Let the real celebration party begin!"

"Big Potatoes" was the speech I gave to close the two-day meeting with the intended purpose of refocusing everyone's attention on moving forward and away from the distraction of the buyout. Secondly, everyone in attendance needed to leave there believing that Godfather's could make it with its new independent ownership.

That was twelve years ago!

BIG POTATOES, GODFATHER'S PIZZA, INC., 1988 CONVENTION

As we come to the end of this 1988 convention, we come to the beginning of a new passage. We must now salute our past and celebrate our future. Our fifteen-year history is now a benchmark by which to measure our future. We have learned some very painful lessons which have made us stronger, not weaker. During the last fifteen years, and for some, even as we speak, we have been down, but never out. Some of you may recall that my grandfather was a Georgia farmer all his life. One of the crops he would raise each year was potatoes. Ironically, he would take a wagon load of potatoes into town to sell at the farmers' market. And he would always get top dollar for a wagon load of potatoes because he would have separated the big potatoes from the little potatoes. But he didn't spend hours and hours of manual labor to separate the potatoes. He would simply take the roughest road into town. By the time he got there, all of the little potatoes would have worked their way to the bottom, while the big potatoes were nicely on the top of the heap. So regardless of the road you had to endure to be here today, as part of the Godfather's Pizza system, as a franchisee, an operator, a restaurant manager, a corporate employee, a supplier, or a distributor, we are all big potatoes.

The road has been rough, the Death Valley years, the deep pan. Moving the corporate office to California and then back to Omaha. Four presidents of the company in three years. Massive advertising by our competitors. But there have been a lot of bright spots along the way—a stronger infrastructure, improved operations, some marketing successes and some marketing disappointments, significant growth in our delivery business, and withstanding another change of ownership. But this time maintaining management stability. The big potatoes have survived despite the roads over which we have traveled and despite everything that has happened to us. We are in a better condition today as a system than we have been in five years.

And now we set sail for our future. We enter this new passage from different backgrounds. With different success and different disappointments. Different experiences and different perspectives and different expectations. But regardless of whether you got here on a little ship, a big ship, a losing ship, a profitable ship, friendship, no ship, or the good ship *Lollipop* . . . we are all in the same boat today. There is room in this boat for only the big potatoes who believe in the future of Godfather's as a system. This boat only has room for those that believe we can withstand the evolution of the world around us and withstand the competitive shots from the "big guys." This boat only has room for those who truly believe the philosophies of focus, unconditional service, and uncompromising quality.

Christopher Columbus believed that the earth was round. And in 1492 he discovered America. His beliefs changed the history of America. The early settlers of our country believed that they wanted freedom from British dominance. They truly believed that they could defeat the British in war to gain their independence. And they in fact did, signing the Declaration of

Independence in 1776. If the original thirteen colonies had not believed in their freedom and their future, we might still have taxation without representation. And instead of the freedom to enjoy coffee breaks, at meetings and conventions, we might have been compelled by British tradition to be having tea breaks. But the thirteen colonies forged ahead as a new nation based on common beliefs. Most of the breakthrough advances in medical and biological science have occurred within the last one hundred years. Scientists attribute this in large part to the naturalist Charles Darwin, who established evolution as a fact, and showed how it was brought about. According to the Encyclopaedia Britannica, before Charles Darwin's work on evolution, biology was in a state of chaos. Darwin's belief changed the course of biological and medical history. Dr. Jonas Edward Salk believed that polio could be prevented, and in 1954 completed the development of a polio vaccine that has virtually eliminated polio in the developed countries of the world. Martin Luther King, Jr., Nobel Peace Prize recipient, believed that although it would take generations to desegregate hearts and minds, we could desegregate our social institutions non-violently. And in 1964, the Civil Rights Act was signed into law. Ever since the end of World War II, Russia and the United States had been toying with outer space exploration. To put a man on the moon. But it wasn't until President John F. Kennedy declared that the United States would put a man on the moon by the end of the decade of the sixties . . . that this became an achievable, mobilized expectation. Kennedy's belief made it possible on July 20, 1969, for Neil Armstrong to take "one small step for man and one giant step for mankind."

McDonald's is considered the greatest chain restaurant success story in our industry, because of size, consistent growth, and consistent philosophy. And although the McDonald brothers, Richard and Maurice, pioneered assembly-line hamburgers, it was the genius of Ray Kroc that created a mega-corporation based on a simple hamburger concept. But according to John Love in his book, *McDonald Behind the Arches,* Ray Kroc's genius was not product innovation, marketing innovation, or even operational innovation; his driving belief was not centered

around food service, table service, counter service, or even win-
dow service. Ray Kroc's genius was his uncompromising belief
in service. Period. And from the first day he set foot onto that
hamburger outlet in San Bernardino, California, in 1954, run by
Dick and Mac McDonald, Ray Kroc recognized and maintained uncompromising beliefs in service—a belief around
which he motivated, harnessed, and sustained a successful
restaurant concept which revolutionized our industry. Although
Domino's is one of our major competitors, one can't help but
give credit where credit is due. Tom Monahan not only believed
in service, but he believed in himself. In the early, early years of
Domino's evolution, Tom Monahan was down more than he
was up, but never out. And although he looked bankruptcy in
the eyes more than once, he believed in his product. He believed
in pizza, and more importantly, he believed in himself.
Monahan's beliefs revolutionized the pizza restaurant industry.

I'm certain that if you could ask Monahan or Ray Kroc,
they would tell you that they didn't do it alone. If you could ask
Kennedy or King, they would say they didn't do it alone.
Neither Salk, Darwin, nor Columbus could have done it alone.
If the original thirteen colonies had not pulled together, they
would never have become the thirteen states of the United
States of America. I'm reminded of the words to a song that I
learned in grade school that says, "No man is an island, no man
stands alone, each man's joy is joy to me, each man's grief is my
own. We need one another so I will defend each man as my
brother; each man as my friend."

As the Godfather's Pizza system sets sail for the future, the
key question is what do you believe? What do you believe about
life? What do you believe about yourself? What do you believe
about other people? And what do you believe about the future
of Godfather's? I can't answer those questions for you. But I can
certainly tell you what I believe.

First, I believe that our Creator put us on this earth to
make a difference—to make a positive impact on the lives of
other people, whether that's in our family, our business, our
church, or our country. If we make a positive contribution, we
will make a positive difference to the people around us. I also

believe that "Life is just a minute, only sixty seconds in it. Forced upon me, can't refuse it, didn't seek it didn't choose it, but it's up to me to use it. I must suffer if I lose it, give an account if I abuse it, just a tiny little minute, but eternity is in it." Secondly, I believe in myself. I grew up in Atlanta, Georgia, during a time when the schools in the South were totally segregated. And in many instances, the black schools were not as well equipped or staffed as the white schools across town. While I was in high school, one of my teachers pointed out that I had, and was getting, and would probably always have an inferior education. Fortunately, there was another teacher who I still remember that told me and others in my class that although our education may have been inferior in some respects, we were not inferior. He also told us we could be whatever we wanted to be in life if we believed in ourselves and were willing to work a little harder to get there.

My parents were from very humble beginnings, with a less than modest lifestyle. In other words, we were technically poor during my early childhood, but my brother and I didn't know it. We did not know we were poor because we had a roof over our heads, and food to eat, and parents, fortunately, who cared about us, and taught us basic values, such as respect, integrity, and consideration for other people. They also sent us both to college, with my mother working domestically, and my father working three jobs simultaneously as a chauffeur, a barber, and a night janitor. Ironically, this night janitor job was with the Atlanta Refrigerated Dough Plant for the Pillsbury Company in the late fifties. I believe in myself, because someone else made a difference in my life.

My belief in myself was inspired not only by my parents and that one teacher who fought inferior surroundings with superior encouragement. I was also inspired by Dr. Benjamin E. Mays, the late president emeritus of Morehouse College, where I attended school, who said, "Failure isn't not reaching your goal, failure is not reaching high enough." But since human nature is the way it is, I was also inspired in other ways. A former boss told me prior to entering Purdue University for graduate school that I probably would not finish the master's degree program because I probably would not be able to maintain the required 3.0 average. He had concluded this based on his assessment of the quality of my educational background rather than on the quality of the man. As a result of his words of "motivation," I finished the master's degree program with a 3.4 grade point average. A former Burger King executive told me that I would not make it in Burger King because they intended to "put me through the wringer" while I was learning operations after leaving a secure Pillsbury VP position. I finished the eighteen-month program in nine months and was assigned to the Philadelphia region as vice president and general manager. I must have been doing something right, because three and a half years later I was asked to become the president of Godfather's Pizza. When I came to Godfather's, some of my then Pillsbury and BK colleagues did not believe we would be here today, talking about our future. Some of our industry associates did not believe that Godfather's Pizza had any "big potatoes." When I came to Godfather's two and a half years ago, I came without a golden parachute. And I came committed to prove the skeptics wrong! And we did!

In February 1988, I was officially informed Godfather's Pizza was going to be sold because it did not fit Pillsbury's strategic future. This was obviously an emotional blow to me and my management team because we were excited about the progress we were making, and the progress and support of you, our franchisees. Since we believed in what we had been doing, we decided to buy the company. Obviously, not everyone believed we would be able to complete the deal because of the hurdles we would have to overcome. It was too highly leveraged, the historical financials were discouraging, and the history of the company was no bed of roses. But we believed we could do it and we did.

My belief in myself is inspired every time someone says "Can't, maybe, I doubt it, or yeah . . . but," because as Henry Ford said, "Whether you believe you can, or you believe you can't, in either case, you're right." I believe in myself because I do not believe in those small, thornless, motionless, spineless, parasitic creatures called yeah-buts.

Thirdly, I believe in other people, other people who are winners. Winners are the right people, with the right stuff, in the right game, with the right coach. I stood before you two and a half years ago and first declared, "Them that's going . . . get on the wagon, Them that ain't . . . get out of the way." I was later informed that some of our constituencies did not believe we were serious about yanking victory from the jaws of defeat. All of you are here today because you were and still are able to dream and commit. I believe in other people who are winners even though it makes me vulnerable to disappointments and sets me up for letdowns. But believing in other people who are winners is a necessary condition for success.

What do you believe? I can't answer that for you. I know that Ron Gartlan believes in Godfather's Pizza. I know that our management group believes in Godfather's Pizza. I also know that many of you believe in Godfather's Pizza and in us. We believe in the future of Godfather's, we believe in ourselves, and we believe in you! It doesn't matter how you got here today, it doesn't matter. Whether you are a small operator or a large operator . . . it does not matter. What we may have disagreed on in the past . . . it doesn't matter. Whether we are franchisee or franchiser, we are all in the same boat. And since we're in the same boat, one does not have to be a rocket scientist to figure out that if we work in the same direction, Godfather's Pizza will become a great ship in that great big sea of restaurants. But only if there are no leaks. And as Ben Franklin said, "A small leak will sink a great ship."

We will be successful with a few good people who have the inner vision to dream. We will be successful with a few good people who have the tenacity to commit. We will be successful with a few "big potatoes" with the desire to compete and make things happen. "There is no joy in easy sailing, when the skies are clear and blue. Nor is there joy in merely doing things that anyone can do. But there is some satisfaction that is mighty sweet to take, when you reach a destination along this journey you thought you'd never make."

We have reached an unexpected destination, but we believe in Godfather's!

As the seventy-fifth chairman of the board and president of the National Restaurant Association in its seventy-five-year history, and having been a member of the board for six years, my first initiative was to highlight the need for us to speak as *one voice*. The ton of regulations, taxes, and fees required at the federal, state, and local level was already mind-boggling, and our elected "leaders" keep passing more and more requirements to try to feed that insatiable appetite for more revenue to accomodate an out-of-control federal spending habit. Although the NRA had fought hard over the years to counter unfair and unnecessary requirements, it is a difficult ongoing battle because of the complexity of the bureaucracy today. The proposed Clinton Health Care Plan (if passed) would have created even more complexity (barriers) and would have been a knockout blow for thousands of businesses. My industry would have been hit especially hard since we are very labor intensive.

Although some legislative proposals impacted some industry segments differently, the proposed health care plan would have impacted most of us the same—badly. Seasoned politicians knew how to maximize the old adage "divide and conquer" so they could do what was politically advantageous. From the day I was installed as president, the one-voice message of my presidency was everywhere—in all my speeches around the country and all association publications and interviews. The one-voice message was a call for action to save free enterprise in America from a knockout blow. The speech I used to deliver that message was called "Save the Frog."

SAVE THE FROG, A MESSAGE ON
RESTORING FREE ENTERPRISE

"We hold these truths to be self-evident, that all Men are created equal. That they are endowed by their Creator with certain unalienable rights. That among these are Life, Liberty, and the Pursuit of Happiness."

Life, liberty, and the pursuit of happiness, the words of our founding fathers, to describe those values most critical to the long-term success of this nation.

Life is short, and in addition to taking from life, we must give back to life. Liberty and freedom, two of the greatest attributes of this great nation, Liberty! Freedom! But greater than freedom itself as a country is America's ability to change. America's early history had a blackened eye because of slavery, but America had the ability to change and rise above slavery.

The pursuit of happiness. Didn't say a guarantee, didn't say it was in the contract that you're gonna be happy. It simply said the opportunity to pursue happiness based upon each individual's desire to apply heart, mind, and back. The heart to have the passion to pursue happiness. The mind to decide that you want to do it. And the back to work as hard as you need to as long as you need to in order to achieve it. That was the premise of our founding fathers. But somewhere along the way, things kind of got off track. Things got a little bit off track in terms of those values and those promises. And one of the big differences today versus the early history of this country is that our elected leaders back then were part-time legislators and full-time employers, citizens. They had real jobs! And when they got through doing the legislative business, which was confined to only a few months out of the year, they'd go back home to their real jobs and relate to real people, talk about real problems, look at real issues, talk about real opportunities, and talk about real pursuit of happiness.

It was in the early thirties that America's greatness was shocked with one of the lowest points in its economic history. All great countries go through some rise and some fall and some decline. And it was in the thirties that this country experienced the Depression. And in an attempt to help those that needed help the most, our government, being a passionate and caring government, wanted to help those to get themselves out of their economic situation. So it was in the early thirties that assistance programs began in this country, starting with Social Security assistance. And when it was originally put forth by the legislators, it was intended to be an assistance mechanism for those that returned after years of pursuing their happiness. And back in 1930, even before they introduced Social Security assistance, a well-intended program, the total cost of all government (federal, state, and local) was ten percent of the Gross Domestic Product, ten percent. And of that ten percent, three of those percentage points were at the federal level; this was in 1930. So back in the thirties when America was showing its compassion to help people, to give people a chance to pursue happiness, we all contributed a little "bite out of our apple." We all shared with those who didn't have as much as we have, as a country. And these assistance programs continued to grow and grow. And back in 1935 when they first passed the Social Security Act, a well-intended program, we were paying three percent of payroll for all of our employees and then the employee was contributing three percent. Today, that number is more than double that. Why? Because in the last sixty years Social Security has gone from being something that is an assistance program to a dependency program to an entitlement program. Entitlement programs weren't defined or even discovered or established in the thirties. They started as assistance, but they evolved to entitlement programs. And instead of our government today being ten percent of our total Gross Domestic Product, thirty percentage points of that fifty percent are going just to the federal level. That's sixty percent of all of the tax level revenue we pay being spent at the federal level today. It was only thirty percent back in 1930; today it's sixty percent.

When Medicare started back in 1965 it was a well-intended assistance program. And our elected representatives told us it would cost six billion dollars to roll out and that in twenty-five years the cost would be twelve billion dollars. But twenty-five years after 1965, the price tag was not twelve billion dollars, it was 107 billion dollars. A 900 percent miss! Oops, we were off by a few decimal points! Back in the early thirties there were no budget deficits. Isn't that a novel idea? There were no budget deficits. The deficits didn't start to grow until we started to allow assistance programs to evolve into entitlement programs. And instead of throwing out the programs that didn't work or modifying programs that needed to be modified, they just continued to grow and eat up more and more of our national revenue. And so today we talk, our legislators talk freely and often about the budget deficit. And the biggest debate going on in the

United States Senate right now today, as I speak and as you listen, is on passing a bill that would force a balanced budget of the United States. This year the budget deficit, the amount we overspend, fell below 300 billion dollars. And if good things continue to happen in the economy, it could get as low as 220 billion dollars. But if we do not change the growth in uncapped entitlement programs, if we as a country do not change our spending habits as a nation, it is estimated by the year 2012, fact, entitlements, and interest on the debt will consume all of our federal tax revenue. So that means we will not have any revenue remaining for defense. The Cold War is over, but you still have some maniacs out there in the world. We would have no money left for education and many other of the discretionary programs if we do not change the course that we're on. And then in 1994, the Mother of all entitlements programs, Health Care Reform. A very noble and worthwhile objective, but a flawed, impractical approach. Because if that approach proposed by the administration had passed with mandates, mandates, mandates, it would have accelerated the bankruptcy date of the United States of America.

Well, some people say, "How did we get into this mess?" And it is a mess. We allowed it to happen, because we elect them, and if we send them to Washington and we don't talk to them, guess what? They will do what is politically right rather than what is economically right. They will do what's good for the party, instead of what's good for the people. It's kind of like the old wives' tale about the frog. If you take a frog and throw him in a pot of boiling water, the frog will jump out. But if you take the frog and put him in a pot of cold water (1935), gradually turn up the heat, little by little, over a long period of time (sixty years), little by little, the frog's body will adjust to that incremental increase of heat, and eventually boil to death. The frog is free enterprise, that boiling heat that we feel as entrepreneurs and businesspeople is the boiling bureaucracy of legislation, taxation, and regulation. As my friend Ted Fowler calls them, the "ations," we've been attacked by the "ations" and don't even realize that the heat's getting hotter.

In 1988, they said, "Let's turn the heat up on the Restaurant Association, let's see if we can't lower business meal deductibility from one hundred percent to eighty percent and see if they notice." And even as an industry, we protested this move because it's simply an unfair tax on our industry, it's just unfair. But our elected representatives, in their infinite wisdom said, "Well, because of the fiscal crisis that we are faced with, we've got to do this, but we won't bother you again." This was in 1988, you've given at the office, so we won't be back to bother you on this issue again.

In 1994, oops, up jumped the devil! Well, since you guys adjusted so easily to change from one hundred percent to eighty percent, well, hell, let's take it to fifty percent. So they turned the heat up just a little bit more on the frog. Made it a little bit harder to start a business. Made it a little bit tougher to stay in business in this industry. And now there's a proposal by the Administration to raise the minimum wage. I have nothing against people pursuing happiness, based upon their heart, their mind, and their back. None of us does. But I have a problem with an unfunded mandate on business. Which is what it is.

And secondly, just to show you the clarity of the logic that we live with in our government, they're working on the wrong problem. There are four million minimum-wage workers in America. Less than one million of them live in a poverty household, which means the total income of the household is less than $13,000 a year. There are 7.8 million people collecting unemployment. There are nine million people on welfare. You are an intelligent business person. Which problem should we be working on? Jobs! And to make matters worse, under the current welfare system, if a welfare person goes out and gets one of these hamburger slinging jobs, as Secretary Reich calls them, then they cut off their Medicaid assistance. That doesn't make any sense. Something is wrong with the system. And so we have allowed the water on the frog to get too hot.

But in 1994, America demonstrated one of its other greatest strengths. And that was its ability once again to change. The unthinkable happened that the political pundits could not predict. That was November eighth. They changed the leadership in Congress. In both houses. Overnight. Shocked the political world and shocked this country. The American people demonstrated once again, the power of the ballot box still rules. And the new Congress and the new leadership have come in and they have said, "We are going to tell the American people the truth about the tragedy, the nature and the size of this problem. And it's going to be painful. But they can't do it without help from us, and encouragement from us to do what is right for this country long-term."

Not all of the people in Washington are bad guys, there are a lot of good guys, there are a lot of good ladies there. But they need the support and encouragement from the citizenry in order to be able to make the kinds of changes that need to be made.

So I encourage you, continue to believe that we can make a difference, because we did and we are.

The second thing we can do about this: make sure that as a businessperson, as an entrepreneur, that you do the basics. Be a registered voter. Vote when it's time to vote. Encourage your employees to vote. Because one of the amazing things that happened in November 1994 was that even though the American people didn't read or understand all of the fine print, they developed a sense that something was going in the wrong direction and they responded. Our privilege and our freedom and our right to vote is one of the greatest privileges that we have in this country and when we do not vote, we risk losing that privilege. Let's do the basics. Contact your elected representatives periodically; they need to hear from you. And yes, it does make a difference.

And number three, we have experienced sixty years of this boiling bureaucracy taking a bite out of our ability to pursue happiness. We've got to bite back. *Better Impact The Elected.* By picking up a phone you can call your representatives and say I agree with a balanced budget amendment. Why? Because we have not as a country demonstrated that we have the fiscal responsibility to do it without a hammer over our head. We haven't done it. The biggest argument that many of the opponents of a balanced budget amendment fear is that it might tie the hands of government. Well, no pepperoni, José. Maybe their hands need to be tied so they can stop taking the money out of my pocket and your pocket.

So yes, America is in a fiscal mess. But it is still the best country in the world. And it is still one of the few countries in the world that can go through the kind of change that we are going through, and the kind of change that we've gone through in the past and lived through it. Joseph Shumpeter, a famous economist, wrote a book in 1942 called *Capitalism, Socialism and Democracy.* And in his book, he stated that the greatest threat to capitalism will not come from its failures, but from its success. And capitalism has been so successful, we've created a mess. And we've got to change it. It's still the greatest country in the world where you can be an entrepreneur. Where you can be whatever you want to be, you can start wherever you want to start, work as hard as you want to work. Who would have thunk it, a young man from Atlanta, Georgia, who had never heard of a pizza could end up running a pizza company one day. Who'd have thunk it! Only in America because of our ability to pursue happiness.

You are the American entrepreneur. We represent that entrepreneurial spirit. That is what this is about when we insist on balancing the budget. That's what this is about when we insist on turning down the heat on the frog. Restoring free enterprise in America. Restoring the ability of people to dream and be able to go and pursue those dreams. Because Rudyard Kipling had it right when he said, "If you can fill life's unforgiving minute with sixty seconds of distance run." We're in a race, folks, we only have a minute to do it. And as Dr. Benjamin E. Mays, who was the president of Morehouse College when I attended there in the late 1960s, said, "It is not a tragedy to not reach your goals, but it is a tragedy to have no goals to reach. It's not a calamity to die with unfulfilled dreams, but it is a calamity to have no dreams to fulfill." Let's restore America's ability to dream, with Life, Liberty, and the Pursuit of Happiness.

IN CLOSING

Public speaking is the number one fear of many Americans. Many people dread having to speak in front of an audience, whereas a few people welcome the experience. Not everyone can become a great speaker, but everyone can become a good speaker with preparation, practice, and the patience to learn from experience. Effective speaking in front of a group of people is as fundamental as language itself: namely, civilization cannot advance without language. You cannot grow as a person and as a professional without developing the better speaker in you. The more speeches you give the better the speaker in you will become, and the better you will be able to use the power of the spoken word to "speak as a leader."

APPENDIX A: QUICK TIPS

Keynote Address

- Think up a memorable title.
- Mention three key points or less.
- Speak for forty-five minutes or less. If a longer speech is requested, then a "great" speech is required.
- Expectations are high since it is a keynote; don't wing it.
- If speech content is new, then practice out loud.
- Avoid distractions just prior to the speech. Find some quiet time.
- Use of audiovisual support materials depends upon content and individual style.
- Being tired is not a good idea.

Create Your Own Tips:

_____

_____

_____

_____

_____

_____

_____

_____

_____

Business Presentation

- Decide on objective and build presentation accordingly.
- Allow and encourage interaction during presentation, but keep it on track and on time.
- If presenting to "superiors" in organization, assume they will interrupt, so be prepared to keep presentation on track.
- Half hour presentation—visual aids optional, takeaway document (executive overview) highly recommended.
- One-hour presentation—visual aids highly recommended. Takeaway document is optional depending upon follow-up required.
- Always present in less than your allotted time unless audience extends time.
- Executive overview can serve as visual aid for audience of two people or less.

Create Your Own Tips:

_____

_____

_____

_____

_____

_____

_____

_____

_____

_____

Banquet or Luncheon Speech

- High "entertainment" value *is* expected.
- Spontaneous humor works best if you are good at it, otherwise, just be pleasant.
- Informational nuggets work best, be succinct.
- Try to connect with something else said or done on the program.
- Never criticize the food or accommodations.
- Relevant personal stories work well, but don't go overboard.

Create Your Own Tips:

_____

_____

_____

_____

_____

_____

_____

_____

_____

_____

_____

_____

_____

_____

_____

_____

Staff Meeting

- Have a written outline of points you want to discuss.
- Think "discussion" rather than presentation—dialogue not monologue.
- Look people in the eye.
- Sit down for small groups, stand for large groups.
- Don't waste your people's time, they have work to do.

Create Your Own Tips:

_____

_____

_____

_____

_____

_____

_____

_____

_____

_____

_____

_____

_____

_____

_____

_____

_____

_____

_____

_____

Committee Report

- Highlights, lowlights, and action items.
- Then, sit down!

Create Your Own Tips:

_____

_____

_____

_____

_____

_____

_____

_____

_____

_____

_____

_____

_____

_____

_____

_____

_____

_____

_____

_____

_____

_____

_____

Press Interview

- Expect the unexpected question.
- There is no such thing as off the record.
- Think sound bites and plan some ahead of time if you know the topic to be discussed.
- Say it over and over.

Create Your Own Tips:

_____

_____

_____

_____

_____

_____

_____

_____

_____

_____

_____

_____

_____

_____

_____

_____

_____

_____

_____

_____

Master of Ceremony

- Your purpose is to *complement* the program not *compliment* yourself.
- Primary responsibilities are opening, continuity, and closing.
- Don't talk too much!
- Know program content and participants ahead of time.
- If you are not a good joke- or storyteller, use relevant quotes.

Create Your Own Tips:

_____

_____

_____

_____

_____

_____

_____

_____

_____

_____

_____

_____

_____

_____

_____

_____

_____

_____

_____

_____

Impromptu Remarks

- Don't experiment; go with what you know.
- One key point or idea is enough, otherwise you are trying to steal the show.

Create Your Own Tips:

_____

_____

_____

_____

_____

_____

_____

_____

_____

_____

_____

_____

_____

_____

_____

_____

_____

_____

Outdoor Event

- Do not try to compete with Mother Nature.
- Be brief, witty, and sit down.

Create Your Own Tips:

_____

_____

_____

_____

_____

_____

_____

_____

_____

_____

_____

_____

_____

_____

_____

_____

_____

_____

_____

_____

_____

_____

All Other Speaking Occasions

• Brevity, message, simplicity, humor.

Create Your Own Tips:

_____

_____

_____

_____

_____

_____

_____

_____

_____

_____

_____

_____

_____

_____

_____

_____

_____

_____

_____

_____

_____

_____

_____

_____

_____

APPENDIX B: PREPARATION SUMMARY

Preparation Summary

Date: _____

Speaking Occasion: _____

    (Quick Tips) _____

_____

Title: _____

Key Points:

    (1) _____

    (2) _____

    (3) _____

Opening:

_____

_____

_____

_____

_____

_____

_____

_____

_____

Closing:

_____

_____

_____

_____

_____

_____

_____

_____

_____

Condiments:

_____

_____

_____

_____

_____

_____

_____

_____

_____

_____

APPENDIX C: EVALUATION FORM

Evaluation Summary

Title: _____

Key Points:

(1) _____

(2) _____

(3) _____

- Evaluate 0–5 with 5 being best

Preparation	Pitch	Pace	Phrasing	Pauses	Projection	TOTALS
□ +	□ +	□ +	□ +	□ +	□ =	□

- Evaluate 0–10 with 10 being best

Inform	Engage	Inspire	Connect	Captivate		
□ +	□ +	□ +	□ +	□	=	□

- Evaluate 0–20 with 20 being best

Overall Performance

□   = □

RATING KEY	
0–2 Painful	7–8 Good
3–4 Pitiful	9–10 Great!
5–6 Average	

TOTAL   = □

TOTAL ÷ 10 = □

APPENDIX D: DEVELOPMENT GUIDE

Chapter 1: Think Before You Speak

1. Select three great leaders to benchmark for your self-improvement.
2. Ask questions of your family and employees every day. Work at becoming a better listener in order to become the best leader possible.
3. Use personal examples to build credibility with the audience.
4. Never be afraid to use examples of risk or failure. Leaders are risk takers.
5. Keep your speech focused on your key message. Edit your speech for critical details and eliminate "nice to know" details.
6. Listen to your employees and remove barriers to their success.
7. Make the time to appreciate the uniqueness of each person in your organization.
8. Use outlines to practice your presentations and speeches.
9. Practice the Rule of Three and brevity with substance.
10. Be yourself and have confidence in your own style.

Notes:

Chapter 2: Message: Choose Your Words Carefully

1. Preparation and diligent practice are the keys to developing the better speaker in you.

 2. Jot down a list of points about the best speech that you have heard recently. Evaluate your speech against these criteria.

3. Your reference library should include a book of famous quotations, an edited collection of famous speeches, and a grammar handbook.

✓ 4. Keep a list of inspirational hideouts and update on a regular basis.

5. Keep a list of your favorite metaphors to illustrate key points about your industry.

✓ 6. Keep a file of editorial cartoons.

7. Never cram for a speech. Schedule preparation and practice time during the day.

8. Visualize yourself in front of the audience each time you practice.

9. Do not speak during a meal. Make your speech before or after the food.

✓ 10. Write the chairperson a thank-you note that acknowledges the speaking engagement and confirms the time, location, audience size, and topic.

Notes:

_____

_____

_____

_____

_____

_____

_____

_____

_____

_____

_____

_____

_____

_____

_____

_____

_____

_____

_____

_____

_____

_____

Chapter 3: Audience: It's Like a Date

1. Carry the contact information with you. Do not pack it in your luggage.

2. Allow enough time to do a sound check and to test the audiovisual equipment.

3. Stay focused on the *message*, *audience* and *delivery* . . . not on being *mad*.

4. Be prepared for common distractions such as babies and cell phones.

5. Be professional and take the high road at all times. Do not allow taunting questions from an audience member to turn into a battle of wills.

6. If the program is disorganized or behind schedule, be alert to the mood of the audience and be prepared to refocus their attention.

7. Be prepared to cut ten minutes from your speech.

8. Remember that there is no such thing as off the record during a media interview.

9. If you want to keep information confidential, keep it to yourself.

10. Develop a repertoire of solid speeches that you can customize for a specific audience.

Notes:

Chapter 4: Delivery: It's Not a Pizza

✓ 1. Unless you have written the speech, never read a speech. Reading pages from a text to an audience is boring.

2. Pace, phrasing, pauses, and pitch are all under your control. Learn how to use them effectively.

3. Practice in front of a large mirror and use a tape recorder to record your voice. Learn what your voice sounds like to others.

4. Nonverbal communication complements the spoken work and can help connect with the audience or disconnect them totally.

5. Posture should be erect but not at military attention.

6. There are at least ten types of speaking occasions. Be sure you have enough material to build a speech for each type.

7. When you are the emcee, your purpose is to complement the program not compliment yourself.

✓ 8. Prepare for panel discussions as you would for a press interview.

✓ 9. When it is "show time," you must be in command of the technical parameters, your message, your body language, and your delivery.

10. Seize the moment to "speak as a leader."

Notes:

APPENDIX E: INTERNET RESOURCE GUIDE

Reference Sites

1. Broadcast.com: This Web site offers four hundred of the world's greatest speeches. Customers may listen to the speeches online or order the CD ROM. www.audionet.com/speeches

2. C-SPAN.org: Watch and listen to speeches from the National Press Club. This Web site includes a calendar of events, video and audio guides, and archived speeches. www.cspan.org/guide/society/npc

3. Freedomvision.com: This Web site includes famous speeches, the Bill of Rights, the Declaration of Independence, and The Word of God. www.freedomvision.com

4. The History Channel is an outstanding source for research. Famous speeches are available in print and audio and video formats. www.historychannel.com

5. The Commonwealth Club hosts interesting speakers on a wide variety of topics. Speeches are available from 1995 through 1998. www.commonwealthclub.org/speeches

6. The History Place is a fabulous Web site. Select a category and search its vast database for great speeches made by men and women throughout history. www.historyplace.com

7. Townhall.com hosts a conservative political forum. In addition to speeches by former presidents and other political leaders, this Web site includes an interactive chat area and coverage of current issues and political opinions. www.townhall.com

8. Miningco.com searches the Net so you do not have to. This Web site is an excellent source for speeches and quotations by writers, historians, politicians, scientists, and other notable speakers. www.miningco.com

9. Great Speeches: This audio Web site contains some of the most famous and infamous speeches of the twentieth century. The speeches are organized by decade beginning with 1940 to present. www.chicago-law.net/speeches

10. Gifts of Speech: This Web site is dedicated to preserving and creating access to speeches made by influential contemporary women. The site has a terrific database. Also, the Nobel Foundation posts copies of all the Nobel lectures by female laureates on this Web site. www.gos.sbc.edu

11. Webcorp's Audio Archive: This Web site is an audio gallery of world leaders. www.webcorp.com

My Favorite Sites:

1.

2.

3.

4.

5.

Corporate Sites

1. The AT&T Newsroom: This Web site features speeches given by AT&T executives from 1995 to present. www.att.com/speeches

2. The DuPont Newsroom: This Web site includes executive speeches, biographies, and position statements. www.dupont.com/corp/whats-new/speeches

3. The McGraw-Hill Companies: This Web site includes

speeches delivered by president and CEO Terry McGraw and other senior executives.
www.mcgraw-hill.com/corporate/news_info/exec_speeches

4. Merrill Lynch: This Web site includes speeches and commentary from executives at Merrill Lynch.
www.merrilllynch.com/woml/commentary/newmenu

5. Intel: This Web site promotes when and where Andy Grove will be speaking next. These speeches cover his computing industry insights delivered from 1997 to present.
www.andygrove.com/intel/people/asg/speeches

6. Microsoft: Speeches by Bill Gates as well as other business presentations are available on this Web site. Powerpoint slides are available for download. This Web site is an excellent resource for training materials and online event information. www.microsoft.com/ms

7. P&G Newsroom: This is the Web site for Procter & Gamble. Speeches by CEO John Pepper and COO Durk Jager are available as well as other remarks by senior executives. www.pg.com/about/news/news

8. FastCompany: Some companies train only their best people. Some use training to weed out people who don't belong. Whom does your company train . . . ? This Web site offers excellent resources about leadership and career management. www.fastcompany.com

9. NikeBiz is the Web site for Nike, Inc. Phil Knight, the founder and CEO, has been the subject of controversy. The Web site contains many resources and its media resource center is a good example of how a company focuses on media relations to keep the media and public informed about issues. www.nikebiz.com/sitemap_main

My Favorite Sites:

1.

2.

3.

4.

5.

U.S. Government and World Organizations

1. The Federal Reserve Board: Speeches given by all members of the Federal Reserve Board are available on this site. Speeches date from 1996 to present. www.bog.frb.fed.us/BOARDOCS/SPEECHES

2. NASA: NASA is committed to spreading the unique knowledge that flows from its aeronautics and space research. This Web site provides the speeches from NASA officials as well as other news and information. www.nasa.gov

3. United Nations: This Web site is maintained by the United Nations Department of Public Information. It is an excellent site for speeches by world leaders and for business and political research. www.un.org

4. The Library of Congress: This Web site offers the historical collections for the National Digital Library. It is a terrific resource for speeches made by Americans throughout our history. www.memory.loc.gov/ammem/amhome

5. The American Experience is a terrific research site for presidential studies. It includes speeches, quotes, and teaching resources. www.pbs.wgbh/amex/presidents

My Favorite Sites:

1.

2.

3.

4.

5.

Leadership Sites

1. Center for Creative Leadership: The center is an international nonprofit educational institution founded in 1970 in Greensboro, N.C. The Web site provides research in the study of managerial practice. www.ccl.org
2. National Association for Community Leadership: This Web site provides resources, information, and national discussion of leadership issues. www.communityleadership.org
3. LeaderNet is a database with over five hundred emerging leaders, representing countries on every continent. This site offers e-mail, newsletters, and discussion groups. www.leadernet.org
4. The James MacGregor Burns Academy of Leadership is a multidisciplinary academic organization that fosters responsible and ethical leadership through scholarship, education, and training and development in the public interest. This Web site includes lectures, research papers, and a community school action program. www.academy.udm.edu
5. Leaders of Tomorrow is a nonprofit organization dedicated to providing education and training in public speaking to students from third grade through college. This Web site offers speeches, videos, workshops, and tips. www.speecheducation.com
6. Future Leaders is a nonprofit organization that will act as

the catalyst that unites current and future leaders. This is an activities-based site designed to help the individual build confidence in leadership skills. www.futureleaders.com

7. Women Leaders Online is the first and largest women's activist group on the Internet—empowering women in politics, media, society, the economy, and cyberspace. www.wlo.org

8. Track & Field Online is a Web site focused on athletic excellence. This Web site features quotes, interviews, discussions, articles, and chats with athletes from a variety of sports. www.trackonline.com

9. Success Coaching is an Internet directory that covers a variety of business fields. This Web site focuses on links to resources on leadership and motivational skills. It has a powerful database and an enormous collection of material. www.selfgrowth.com/success

My Favorite Sites:

1.

2.

3.

4.

5.

Speaking as a Leader

1. Abraham Lincoln Online: This site features the speeches by Abraham Lincoln.
   www.netins.net/showcase/creative/lincoln/speeches

2. The Speeches of Winston Churchill: This audio site features the pre-WWII speeches of Winston Churchill.
   www.winstonchurchill.org/

3. Rainbow/Push Coalition: This Web site features an audio

library of speeches by the Reverend Jesse Jackson as well as live broadcasts and interviews. www.rainbowpush.org

4. Gandhi: Mohandas Karamchand Gandhi (1869–1948) was born in Porbandar, a village in Gujarat province in India. He became the father of Indian independence and one of the greatest spiritual and political leaders of modern times. His teachings have inspired countless movements and individuals. This Web site offers surviving original audio recordings of this great leader. www.harappa.com/sounds/gandhi

5. Dr. Carl Sagan inspired and touched the lives of many people. This Web site is a tribute site with speeches and quotes from Dr. Sagan. www.io.com

6. Mother Teresa dedicated her life to the poor. This Web site offers talks, quotes, speeches, words, and video of Mother Teresa. www.tisv.be/mt/life

7. The Albert Einstein Home Page has a terrific database available for research. The site includes quotes and speeches. www.humboldt1.com/~gralsto/einstein

8. Hour of Decision is the Web site that offers the speeches and sermons by the Reverend Billy Graham. www.hod.billygraham.org

9. Let's Talk Business Network includes the Entrepreneur's Hall of Fame, a Web site dedicated to entrepreneurs. This Web site is rich in database resources. It offers biographies, quotes, and speeches. www.ltbn.com

10. The Consumer Electronics Manufacturing Association sponsors a CEO summit. This Web site is an excellent collection of resources for the electronics industry. It offers interviews, speeches, and chats. www.cemacity.org

My Favorite Sites:

1.

2.

3.

4.

5.

Speechwriting Resources

1. IdeaBank: This database is available as a subscription service only. However, free trials are available for professionals. Subscribers include business executives, speechwriters, editors, government officials, public relations executives, librarians, and clergy. This Web site contains a large collection of quotations, anecdotes, books, proverbs, and humor. Find historical "pegs" for your presentation in the History Today file. www.idea-bank.com

2. Speech Writing Tips and Resources: This Web site is a collection of useful links. www.speeches.com/gentips

3. The HTML Writers Guild is the world's largest international organization of Web authors with over eighty-five thousand members in more than one hundred thirty nations worldwide. The Web site exists to assist its members in developing and enhancing their capabilities as Web authors. This a terrific Web site for learning skills in order to publish information in today's high-tech world. www.hwg.org

4. Inkspot is a comprehensive writing resource and community. This Web site offers market information and tips on improving your writing abilities. It includes interviews with professional editors, networking opportunities, and a guide to the best resources for writers on the Net. www.inkspot.com

My Favorite Sites:

    1.

    2.

    3.

    4.

    5.

BIBLIOGRAPHICAL REFERENCES

Barker, Joel Arthur. *Paradigms.* New York: HarperCollins, 1992.

Barker, Julie *Successful Meetings.* "Three Spellbinders Who Inspire, Motivate and Change Attitudes." June 1998.

Cain, Herman. *Leadership Is Common Sense.* New York: Lebhar-Friedman Books, 1998.

Fast, Julius. *Body Language.* New York: M. Evans, 1970.

Johnson, James Weldon. *The Creation.* Boston: Little Brown, 1993.

Phillips, Donald T. *Lincoln on Leadership.* New York: Warner Books, 1992.

INDEX